If writing seems hard, it's because it is hard.

It's one of the hardest things that people do. ~ William Zinsser

Writing a book is a horrible, exhausting struggle, like a long bout with some painful illness. One would never undertake such a thing if one were not driven by some demon whom one can neither resist nor understand. ~ George Orwell

You can't wait for inspiration.

You have to go after it with a club. ~ Jack London

Previous Works by the Author

M.A. Lee: Historical Mysteries & Suspense, all with a Dash of Romance

Hearts in Hazard Series, books 1 to 12 available

1 ~ *A Game of Secrets*

2 ~ *A Game of Spies*

3 ~ *A Game of Hearts*

4 ~ *The Danger of Secrets*

5 ~ *The Danger for Spies*

6 ~ *The Danger to Hearts*

7 ~ *The Key to Secrets*

8 ~ *The Key for Spies*

9 ~ *The Key for Hearts*

10 ~ *The Hazard of Secrets*

11 ~ *The Hazard for Spies*

12 ~ *The Hazard for Hearts*

Into Death series

Digging into Death: Has the love of her life beguiled her straight into death?

Christmas with Death: Christmas is for miracles, merriment, and murder.

Portrait with Death: Can an artist avoid death when murder paints with blood?

Also Look for Writing Guides by M.A. Lee, including the **Discovering Your Writing** series.

Think like a Pro

by M.A. Lee

Think like a Pro Writer ~ 1

Think like a Pro: New Advent for Writers

Part of the Think like a Pro Writer series

Copyright © 2017 M. A. Lee / Emily R. Dunn & Writers' Ink

First electronic publishing rights: 2017

2nd Edition: 2023

NOTE FROM THE AUTHOR

This book is a work of non-fiction. Any names, characters, places, and incidents of fiction and nonfiction are cited by the author merely as explanation. Any persons or entity, existing or dead, are also cited by the author for the purposes of explanation. The author does not have any control over and does not assume any responsibility for third-party websites or their content.

Published in the United States of America.

Cover Design by Deranged Doctor Design

winkbooks@aol.com

www.writersinkbooks.com or

The Write Focus

Table of Contents

Think like a Pro ... 3

Introducing Think like a Pro: New Advent for Writers ... 7

My Journey ... 7

The Crossroad ... 9

The Transformation ... 10

Be a Writer ... 11

The 7 Lessons ... 12

Chapter 1 ~ One Scary Word :: Deadlines ... 13

First Step to a Deadline ... 14

3 Deadline Tricks ... 14

Develop Three Sets of 7 for Success.   21

An Official Deadline Creator for Newbie Writers: NaNoWriMo ... 28

Wrapping Up ... 32

Chapter 2 ~ One Latin Phrase :: Nulla Dies Sine Linea ... 33

We must WRITE EVERYDAY 33

Plan to Write / Write to the Plan ... 35

Plan the Work to Work the Plan ... 38

A Plan Creates Magic ... 40

Wrapping Up ... 41

Chapter 3 ~ One Guiding Decision :: Plot It ... 43

Building Story ... 43

Building Avant Garde ... 44

Building Plot: Booker's 7 Types of Plot ... 45

A Detailed Look at the 7 Plot Types ... 46

The Key to all 7 Plot Types ... 55

Five Methods for Plotting ... 57

Plot: a Slugfest ... 63

Chapter 4 ~ One Ancient Greek :: Aristotle Rocks Characters ... 69

Aristotle on Structure ... 70

5 Essentials in Structure to Reveal Character … 71

Aristotle on Characters … 77

Wrapping Up … 85

Chapter 5 ~ One Simple Injunction: Writer's Block Doesn't Exist … 86

The Heretical Belief … 87

The Truth about Writer's Block … 88

Writer's Refusal … 91

Writer's Procrastination … 98

Writer's Inertia … 102

Wrapping Up … 106

Chapter 6 ~ One Slice of Advice :: Let it Sleep … 107

Let It Sleep … 107

13 Ways to Spark Creativity … 109

While It Sleeps … 113

The End of the Season of Sleep … 115

Chapter 7 ~ One Resolution :: Be a Writer … 117

Juggling … 118

Mantras … 118

The # 1 Resolution … 119

Closing … 127

Check out these releases from Writers Ink Books … 132

Releases from M.A. Lee … 137

Fantasy from Writers Ink Books … 140

Introducing *Think like a Pro: New Advent for Writers*

Talk the walk. Walk the talk. Which is better?

Hobbyist. Professional. Who is better?

Think like a Pro: New Advent for Writers started as a series of blogs when I considered my own learning curve from "talking the walk" of claiming to be a writer to "walking the talk" of being a writer.

A retrospective self-analysis was necessary to understand my transformation from wannabe to big-bee. As I considered that transformation, I understood that what I had done was change my mind-set. I stopped thinking of my writing as entertainment / hobby and began pursuing it as a means to an end.

Think / Pro became my mantra. How did I do it?

How does anyone change their mindset from "this is my hobby" to "this is my job"?

We all have our wants and our dreams. How do we take those dreams and transform them into reality?

My Journey

Let me digress.[1]

---

[1] Digressions do teach—although my students never realized it until I pointed to that digressive story several days later. If you want to avoid this section, please use the **Table of Contents** to leap to the **"Be a Writer"** section in this Introduction or head straight to **Chapter 1 ~ One Scary Word :: Deadlines**. I share it for the sole purpose of proving my point about drifting through life, looking forward to a dream that I could have turned into a reality much more quickly than I did.
You don't have to read it. It is a teaching digression, if you will, the story of my journey merely as explanatory information.

For many, many years, writing stories was no more than my dream.

Just as artists and garage wood-workers and amateur photographers dream of turning their hobby into a money-making endeavor, I dreamed of selling my writing. "Professional writer" was the job title I wanted.

But I didn't seek that dream. I didn't take my dream seriously.

Shame on me.

Oh, I wrote.

I drifted off to write stories whenever I wanted to escape day-to-day reality. Distractions popped up, and I followed their pied-piper song. Stories started up but never ended.

Occasionally, I would set writing goals, but I wasn't serious about them. If I missed my deadline, I just moved it. My goals stayed nebulous, so I could re-define what achievement meant.

Every writer craves a huge bank of hours to devote to writing. Along with that, I claimed frustration with the little hour or two I managed to squeeze out around TV watching and voracious reading. Worse, when I managed to achieve an afternoon for that bank of hours, I frittered the time away, dabbling at this, at that, at the other, and another.

Dozens of stories started up. When new ideas came up, I dropped the old for the new shiny. I mastered file organization.

Whatever book I was reading became the genre of my writing.

I attended writing meetings and conventions; I paid dues to various writing organizations. Over the years I learned many, many techniques and methods and devices. But I didn't take those lessons to heart.

I called myself a writer. And I *was growing* as a writer. My files gradually filled up with finished manuscripts and rejection letters. Yet I drifted like a dandelion seed, purpose-filled but unrooted, floating with the vagaries of the wind.

I knew about plot: I was an English teacher, for heaven's sake. Story basics were my bread and butter. Yet never once did I apply classroom analysis to my own characters and plot.

With a basic untrained talent for clear writing, I thought that was enough. Reading gazillions of words of fiction had me thinking I had an intuitive recognition of characters and plot—which was far, far away from an understanding of character development and plot structure.

I refused the excuse of writer's block to my students, but I would go months without writing. I became sadder and sadder without any creative outlet. When I managed to kindle creativity, I let other influences distract from my writing habit.

When I finished something and corrected it (thinking that line editing was enough), I shoved the manuscript into a submission package then waited for a response. A professional writer would have turned to the next project. I waited. I stayed focused on that project while it was out to the agents or editors—until it returned so many times that I admitted its failure. Only then did I move to the next idea.

I allowed distractions; I caused distractions.

This is the number one problem that hobbyists have: they have a dream, but they don't stick to the dream in order to turn it into reality. Hobbyists drift away from their focus then come back. They dabble in it. They piddle with it. They fritter time away doing it—but they never DO it.

Hobbyists want the dream of being a professional. They just don't want it enough.

I knew how to be a professional at my job, the job that claimed so much of my writing time. Yet if professional writer was my dream, why wasn't I pursuing it with the same intensity?

Obviously, I didn't want my dream enough.

The Crossroad

A handful of years ago I saw a major life crossroad coming up.

Everyone has crossroads.

We reach a junction of life. We see our past with its equal moments of pride and embarrassment, narrow escapes and glittering achievements.

Ahead of us are three or more roads. Which one do we choose?

Most crossroads strike without warning. Occasionally, only occasionally, the crossroad takes a little time to reach us: engagement and marriage, a career move or advancement, a complete career change, moving to another location hundreds or thousands of miles away, retirement—all the things that business institutions call "life events".

The lucky ones of us see those crossroads coming. Often, though, most of us never have time to choose our next road: we just hope for the best as we drive on, choosing our next turn on little more than a whim and a flashing thought.

I was lucky. I was unstressed and healthy, clear thinking and emotionally stable. For most of us, the confluence of all four is rare.

I peered into the next couple of years and saw the approaching life change. For once, I had the good sense to ask myself, "Where do I want to be when I reach that crossroad?"

And I remembered my dream, the dream that had begun to haunt me: Professional Writer.

The years had slipped past since I first declared my dream. I learned and dabbled, experimented and experienced. I don't regret those lost years. After all, we're placed where we're supposed to be—just as I hope this book is a helpful lesson for others.

Yet when I saw that crossroad ahead, I opened my eyes and my mind, and I decided to do it.

I would *Be a Writer*. I needed to think like a professional writer in order to become a professional writer.

The Transformation

My first step was to create a new mantra: Dream it. Believe it. Do it.

Going professional meant treating my writing like a business: Writers Ink was born.

Businesses need websites: www.writersinkbooks.com

Electronic publishing was no longer new, so ebooks would be my marketplace. No longer would I pursue traditional publishers. I would be an Indie Writer. I would write what I wanted to read.

A dream needs a purpose. I created a plan and resolved to follow it. From the stack of finished manuscripts that were unaccepted by the Trad Publishers, I picked up two to work on. Over the next half-year, I would polish them for publication.

With a dream and a purpose, I started.

A steep learning curve ensued.

- I learned that a purpose is not a plan, and a plan is not a calendar.
- Each manuscript became a project, divided into workable increments with deadlines for each, to be completed without taking long breaks.
- Gaps in my knowledge about indie publishing surfaced, requiring research.
- The manuscript requirements for electronic publishing had to be found and studied and implemented. This learning curve was easier than I thought it would be.
- Finding a cover designer was not the easy search that I had anticipated. My hunt took 18 months. I had to start setting aside money to pay for covers (and to this day I use professional cover designers for my fiction but a computerized cover creator for my non-fiction).
- Marketing became a chief frustration. Discoverability became a new buzzword, one that I'm still working on.
- As part of marketing, I discovered that publishing three manuscripts was much better than sending the lone title into the vast marketplace. Thus, in addition to polishing two manuscripts, I had to write a third one, and everything I had learned about deadlines and determination came into the battle of those eighteen months of sketching and research and polishing and drafting and revising and hunting and re-planning and re-purposing and editing and correcting.

The crossroad came closer. I checked that I was in the right lane.

I kept my head focused on the dream and starting cutting more distractions. I started following a plan. I started re-thinking the way I looked at writing.

The crossroad loomed. I watched it come and started publishing, those first three books, then another and another and then three more.

And I blazed through the junction.

Be a Writer

I'm here now, living the dream. I still have lessons to learn. I still have stories to tell.

Here's the key.

Writing is no longer a hobby. I'm walking the walk. I'm a Pro.[2] A Pro

---

[2] Indie, yes, but don't ever let anyone tell you that's not good enough. From little acorns mighty oaks grow; from small businesses come larger ones.

doesn't think like an amateur. A Pro knows deadlines and determination.

Talent is helpful, but writing is a craft. A craft can be learned and improved upon. A Pro will do the work in order to improve.

This book is to help others learn to *Think / Pro*. Its lessons are for anyone wanting to start a small business. They apply far beyond the world of writing. Here they are:

The 7 Lessons

Use deadlines. [chapter 1 = One Scary Word]

Work every day. [ch.2 = One Latin Phrase]

Models and patterns help. [ch.3 = One Guiding Decision]

Learn from those who've gone before. [ch.4 = One Ancient Greek]

Give up the excuses. [ch.5 = One Simple Injunction]

Creativity can be sparked. [ch.6 = One Slice of Advice]

Stay determined. [ch.7 = One Resolution]

Read the chapters. Understand their lessons. And convert from a wannabe to a big-bee Pro.

Chapter 1 ~ One Scary Word :: Deadlines

Ah, the dreaded deadline.

I start with deadlines because they are the single-most important key to success.

Every project has a deadline.

Without a deadline looming—harvest, publication, trial date, gallery opening, season start—without this coming date, nothing would get done.

Deadlines get things done.

Harvest deadline > first frost.

Trial Date > the starting date is set by the judge.

Gallery Opening > set by the gallery owner.

Season start > set by the powers that be of football, soccer, basketball, baseball, etc.

Publication date? Well, babe, you set that.

Hate them, despise them, loathe them, want to shoot them: deadlines are necessary.

And we get no reprieve from a deadline. When we don't meet it, it still stands; we've just passed it and know—KNOW—we are behind.

First Step to a Deadline

Setting a **Deadline** is the first procedure[3] that anyone starting a project must determine.

Very simply, a deadline means "When is this sucker due?"

For indie writers, their novels and stories and blogs could be due whenever. But "whenever" is NOT thinking like a pro. For ANY person anticipating the start of a new job, new career, new life, the deadline will not be a "whenever" drift-into dream. Deadlines mean reality will come. Deadlines mean, "Here's the date. Let's go."

Pro career professionals, pro artists, pro athletes: they all know when their project deadline is. For the career professional, the deadline is the day the case starts or the client arrives. The pro artist anticipates the gallery preparation. The canvases and prints must be ready before the gallery does any set-up. Pro athletes train for the first day of training camp which comes long before the start of the official pre-season games which lead to the real season, and all of those lead to the Bowl games and major tournaments that culminate an athletic season.

And then, gallery showing and seasons over, case done, projects complete, everyone looks at the next project.

For indie writers who want to go pro, publication is the deadline. Publication is not a nebulous dream. We're turning dreams into reality. The time for drifting and dreaming is over. We have determination, and determination means we set **deadlines**.

3 Deadline Tricks

Here are 3 Must-Have Deadline Tricks, so-called because they magically turn dreams into reality.

These Deadline Tricks work not only for writers but for anyone tackling major projects. While these are separated for writing projects, other projects can and should be broken into major areas.

Training the body is not merely running. For full fitness, the different muscle groups are considered. Overworking the body can be as dangerous as not working the body at all. And anything put into the body is extremely important to its performance. Diet, fluid intake, avoidance of EMFs, all are just as important as any group of exercises.

---

[3] Procedure :: a series of steps followed in a regular definite order / Merriam-Webster online.

Artists need to know the skills for their art, naturally. But creating a gallery showing is in many respects telling a story. What is the overall impression? How do the first canvases create the first perspective? How will that perspective change as attendees move through the gallery? Which techniques will work best where?

For career professionals, newbies have all their official training. Then come the soft skills: people skills and daily work coping skills and the unseen, almost covert processes that run a business. What tools are needed? How best to use those tools? When do those tools not work? When approaching a project, especially the way a lawyer does, what is the end result? What are the steps to achieve that end result? Or a doctor's diagnoses: when can she trust what she knows, when should she doubt what she knows, and when should she research more?

Writers write.

"But how many days do I set aside to reach that deadline?" you ask.

I won't be like other people who would answer, "You'll learn." Or even cruelly, "You'll know when you've done it a few times." We're starting! How can we know before we've done it?

Keep reading. I'll explain how to build your deadline. For now ~

Here are the 3 Must-Have Deadline Tricks. Ready?

Trick 1 :: Determine your Daily Work Routine

Your Work Routine means how much you can reasonably accomplish when all works well.

That sentence is important. Read it again. I'll wait.

Now~let's parse the important elements.

Key Words: "Reasonably" and "When all works well". This is not "when everything's going great". Determine a basic meet-able goal. For writers, this is an achievable daily word count. For athletes, the number of hours that can be devoted to training on each day. Even artists consider the amount of work on a canvas that can be achieved over several days. Lawyers consider the time needed for preparation of the upcoming case: witness statements, interviews, official depositions, law research, scene mapping, and on and on.

Note Well: In the examples above (lawyer, athlete, etc.), all of the goals are TIME-BASED. Your *reasonable* writing goal is not a sprint, not a squeezed-in segment. If you had an uninterrupted hour, how many words can you *reasonably* churn out? How many hours can you *reasonably* work each day? How many days per week do you lose to other, more pressing concerns?

Do the Math: What is the word count for your project? For writers, novels and novellas and short stories and scripts and blogs, all these have specific word counts[4]. Genres have specific word counts. Are you writing an epic fantasy of 120K? Are you writing a romantic comedy of 45,000 words? When you know what you need to write, you have your first working number.

Divide the total expected word count by your daily writing goal. This gives you an estimate of the number of days needed to complete the project. (Yes, I hate math, too!)

Trick 2 :: Determine the Steps Needed to Achieve your Goal

Just like any project, writing has a lot of hidden steps that outsiders never see. Writing is much more than pouring the words onto the page. Novels, especially, are very involved and very messy projects.

Here are the 10 Top Factors to consider when starting a writing project. These factors build a novel. Ignore them at a great cost.

Factor for the Following~

1) Prep-time to set up the necessary background information. Characters are the foundation of the whole project. Spend the time creating the most important ones. Use your Table of Contents to flip to this chapter's section called *Develop your Characters* if you can't wait. This little manual also has a second take on characters, based on Aristotle, in *Chapter 4 ~ One Ancient Greek.* At the beginning, a well-considered character takes between one and two hours (generally) while a secondary character (foil or blocking figure) will take less than a half-hour. Antagonists[5] are just as important as protagonists. Walk-ons should be five minutes.

2) Building the book prep-time. Before you ever start the "official manuscript", spend some time knowing if you have a book or not.[6] Use something similar to the 12 Key Pillars of Novel Construction[7] or my own

---

[4] https://thewritelife.com/how-many-words-in-a-novel/
[5] Do not confuse antagonistic minions with the antagonist.
[6] This piece of advice comes from Jenny Crusie, and I spent YEARS not realizing what she meant.
[7] The 12 Key Pillars of Novel Construction, C.S. Lakin ::

Plot 7 to determine if this "idea" you have will actually turn into a book. The Plot 7 is in this chapter's section called *Develop your Plot* which you can find in the TOC, again, if you're impatient. And, of course, *Chapter 4 ~ One Ancient Greek* presents Aristotle's take on plot through character, quite different from the 12 Pillars and the Plot 7. The 12 Pillars and the Plot 7 take me three to five days, sometimes more. Once, I did it in one day, but nothing else was going on that day. Wouldn't you know it? I had to come back a week later and add more; the creative side of my brain needed percolation time.

3) Research prep, including world-building. World-building is more than setting, just as setting is more than time and place. Setting is also culture: think of the many cultures in a high school ~ jock, band geek, drama nerd, hoodies, scared newbies, drifters and go-getters, and more. World-building creates a map of the immediate place as well as the larger world. Contemporary writers may seem to have it easy; however, the rapid pace of technology will quickly cause anachronisms.

What are the ethnic groups? The governmental entities? The religions? The rebellions, themselves a fanatical religion?

The social structure? It's usually a pyramid, with the mass of people at the bottom. How is that mass of people controlled?

The educational structure? The narrow-minded and the hidebound? The level of technology? If you were going to match to an actual historical era, what tech will be available?

What tech has been lost? The ancient Greeks forgot how to write. The water wheel had to be re-invented. The Chinese had black powder long before Europe did, but the Europeans developed cannons while the Chinese developed firecrackers and rockets. How do different areas in your world use the same tech in different ways?

The flow of the rivers? The run of the mountain ranges? The forests and the lack of forests? The swamps, literal and figurative?

And more, much more.

4) Writing the Basics. This is your Math Equation from **Trick 1**. To that answer, add the following ~ How many pages will you devote to each chapter[8]? To answer this question, list the logical sequence that moves the

---

https://www.amazon.com/Key-Pillars-Novel-Construction-Blueprint-ebook/dp/B00T0NJ6RQ

[8] Generally, your chapters are main plot points which might take three to five chapters

protagonist from Plot Point 1 to 7 or through the Pillars.

When you consider the minor characters such as Seeming Allies and Foils, what gaps remain in your character list? Who do you still need to add in?

The scene-sequence will help you determine your chapters. Chapters may have three or more scenes.

5) Planning at the Mid-Point ~ because "life" happens even in stories and blogs. Characters change. The plot falls apart. Your mind throws you a twist that improves everything you're doing. That fortunate twist unfortunately requires re-writing and adding and gutting. Mid-Point planning may take two to five days.

6) Revising ~ BTW, will you revise as you go or revise at the end? Both? Fair Warning: Revising adds chaos back into a manuscript that you thought had become orderly.

7) Editing ~ developmental editing, content editing, line editing.

8) Cover development ~ the graphics and the blurb

9) Correcting the editing. Keep your fingers crossed. However, you may wind up at Factor 3 again.

10) Getting everything ready for publication ~ the "yippee" step. But formatting the manuscript can be a beast. A conquerable beast, but you need to factor a couple of days, at minimum.

11)

Trick 3 :: Count the Days for the Whole Project

Get out a calendar. A physical calendar, not a digital one. Don't have one? Print one. Draw one.

You may be totally digital. I like digital. Yet blocking out a calendar is best done on paper. Trust me on this one. That small screen hides things and hides the big picture.

A deadline is Big Picture.

---

to cover. Consider that a manuscript "usually" has between 200-250 words per page. Some chapters run from 7 to 21 pages in length, depending on the type of work it is. William Faulkner and James Patterson have had chapters only a page in length (Faulker, in *As I Lay Dying*, actually had only one short sentence, "My mother is a fish", as a chapter.) Programs like *Scrivener* have an arbitrary scene length and number-of-scenes per chapter length. Life, though, is rhythmic, with ebbs and flows of less and more. This is a guesstimate. Build in extra if you don't like writing tons of words as you draw closer to the deadline. Some people say they work best at the last minute. Having dealt with procrastinating students for years, however, I will tell you that your best work is never rushed.

It's like depending on a small-screen map-app vs. seeing a plat of the roads you will actually drive. Map-apps are convenient, but it's easy to get lost unless you are a complete robot. Not that I'm prejudiced against robots.

That calendar, in your hands, creates a mental process that begins a brain change. When we're moving from drifting dream to determined reality, brain changes are necessary.

Start blocking off days to create your **deadlines**.

This many days for Factors 1 to 3. So many days for Factors 4 and 5. And so on.

Start running the Word Count Days.

Give yourself two handfuls of days to fall behind for unforeseen circumstances: like the flu, like a car breaking-down, like a friend coming to visit, like four weddings and a funeral. Remember ~ "life" happens.

How many days for 6? Expect problems.

Factor for Editing, #7. How many times? How many people? OMG, how many interruptions? And definitely be a Pro here: if you ship out your editing, what will you work on while you're waiting for the manuscript to return home?

Find some trust-worthy First Readers (also called Beta Readers) and factor the time needed for them to help you at this point. Don't give them the chaos, please. Give them what you think is a finished manuscript, and ask them to be brutal.

You may want to ask yourself "Do I need a developmental editor? Do I need a content editor?" Yes, you need a line editor. Spell-check and grammar reviewers don't catch everything. *Vial vs. Vile,* anyone?[9]

Factor for 8. The blurb is extremely important. It's more important than your first chapter. How many days did you set aside for the first chapter? Schedule that number of days for your blurb. Devote a solid day to the tagline, a short sentence that will capture your story for the reader. While you're working on and re-working on and revising your blurb and tagline, take a break from words to consider what you want the cover elements to be. Image is more important than words[10].

---

[9] http://writersinkservi.com/2016/09/09/mistakes-so-bright-ive-got-to-wear-shades/
[10] If words were more important than images, books would outsell films and TV.

Factor for 9. When you spend sufficient time on Factors 1 to 4, correcting the edited manuscript should fly. If you're a pantster, editing shows up problems that will affect the entire manuscript. If you're a planner who's also a pantster, like me, you'll have a few problems but not the major chaos that I've heard some people talk about. (And I'll admit to a little gloating that I didn't have that back-end chaos. Nope, my chaos is at the beginning.)

Factor for 10.

Mark everything on your paper calendar. Did you see birthdays show up? Any major events, like graduations or weddings, anniversaries, holidays, vacations, etc.? Yes, I know, but we must remain loyal to family and friends. Don't schedule through them; schedule around them. By some fortunate circumstance, if you find you get in unscheduled words on Christmas Day, consider those words your Christmas gift to yourself.

Now, pull out that handy digital calendar and input the major deadline dates:

- Finishing Prep
- Finishing Draft
- Manuscript Finished
- Revision Done
- Editing Completed
- Corrections Over
- Cover back
- Publish!

It would be LOVELY if all you had to do was start with the first sentence.

Some people can do this; many can't.

A lot of pantsters who never finish need to reverse engine and do a little planning before they write the first sentence.

A lot of plotters who never finish overload their engine with too much planning and lose all interest before they reach the middle.

Don't start with a blank idea of where you're going, AND don't start with so much prepped that the spark of creativity is overshadowed.

Develop Three Sets of 7 for Success.

Develop 7 Characters

Devote pages to your character descriptions: tape a photograph to each character's page.

~ Two Main Characters ~

Protagonist(s) :: goal / motivation / conflict.[11] The goal is what the character most wants in life. The motivation is the reason for the goal: usually something to be escaped through gaining something else. Escape is often motivated by a past trauma. Conflict is what prevents achieving that goal, what fear blocks the protagonist, and what external enemy stands in the way.

Describe them physically, intellectually, emotionally. What do they want? What's in their way? Where do you want them to wind up?

Antagonist:: GMC, also. We may discover things about our protagonists by learning the reason the antagonist is in conflict with them.

Repeat the same templates and information that you used for the protagonist. Your antagonist is as important—and many say MORE important—than your protagonist.

~ Two More Essential Characters ~

Confidante:: Who will keep your protagonist going when s/he is mired in the mud? The confidante is the best friend, the one who knows the protagonist's secrets (not the heart secrets, but all of the others).

Describe them. How did they become a confidante? Will they remain a confidante? If no, why not? Will your antagonist have a confidante? Know their wants and conflicts and end result.

What commonality ties the Confidante to the Protagonist? GMC, also.

Seeming Ally:: The SAlly character is more important than the confidante. This is the archetypal shapeshifter: the character who begins trusted but then is not. The alternative form of the shapeshifter is to begin as UN-trusted and then become so. A SAlly, however, is purely devious and manipulative.

---

[11] … and if you haven't read Deb Dixon's book *Goal, Motivation, & Conflict*, this challenge is an excellent opportunity to put her lessons into action.

You may want to research the cunning and manipulative sociopath if you are seeking a villainous character in addition to your antagonist. The sociopath would undermine your protagonist until the protagonist understands just what the SAlly is.

When will the Seeming Ally turn on the P? What first reason will the SAlly give? What is the real reason?

Is the SAlly going against the P on his/her own? Or is the SAlly working for the A and has been all along?

Most definitely, the SAlly needs a GMC breakdown.

~ 4 Required Character Sets ~

Blocking Figures:: These are especially strong if they are family or close friends of the P. They get in the way, for the best intentions. Love and guilt are strong motivators for the P.

Often well-intentioned family and friends see the protagonist on a different path than the one s/he has chosen. For this reason, they will actively block the protagonist from the desired goal.

These characters can supply guilt as the protagonist is pulled between the old, easy path and the newer, challenging path that leads to her/his desire.

Foils:: characters who mirror the protagonist and proceed along the same path only to fail, often tragically. They foreshadow what may happen to the protagonist if s/he does not make the dynamic changes necessary.

The protagonist's dynamic changes are tied to three major discoveries: the desired goal rather than end result, the betrayal of the SAlly, and the true heart of the antagonist. Learning these three clarifies the nobler path of the protagonist. Otherwise, s/he is merely a foil.

Foils reflect one or several of the personality traits of the P. These are the characters who can be associated with the P then killed off to create a suspenseful belief in the audience that the P will be killed off as well.

Walk-Ons and Cameos:: Walk-on characters provide information or do minor errands; hangers-on who have a single purpose.

Cameos are characters you want to highlight, especially if they're part of later or previous books.

Similar to Walk-Ons, Cameos should not take an active role and interfere with the protagonist as the main character. However, a Cameo can be a blocking figure, a foil, a confidante, or even a SAlly (as long as the Cameo remains true to the personality you created for him previously).

Develop the Plot 7

Many different versions of plot structures abound. Seven types of plot as well as five methods of plotting are presented for you in *Chapter 3 ~ One Guiding Decision :: Plot It.*[12] Then we have Aristotle's essentials for any plot through character in *Chapter 4.*

I sometimes think there are as many different versions of plot as there are adaptations of Pachelbel's "Canon in D". **Plot 7**, my own version, is just another adaptation.

When you are starting the manuscript and considering how the deadline will work, you are not really concerned—not at the very beginning—with the complete structure of the novel. Deal with the complete novel when you know whether or not you have a story.

PLOT 7 will tell you if a story's there, or warn you if you just have a burgeoning idea still in the incipient stage. About 25 to 40 pages is sufficient.

Here's Plot 7. These are out of order for a reason. Follow this order and re-arrange when you're finished with this white-hot creativity. Knowing the Plot 7 gives you an idea about how to sequence and develop the whole structure.

~ Open and Close ~

~~ Plot 1 = Beginning.

How are you going to introduce your protagonist?

How will the protagonist meet the antagonist? Why will the antagonist be similar to the protagonist? How will the antagonist be different (this is KEY)?

What do you want the protagonist to be doing when the reader first meets her/him?

What exhibits the protagonist's dissatisfaction with life as it currently is?

What represents the dear desire that the P wants so very much?

~~ Plot 2 = Ending.

---

[12] Time, once again, for that handy-dandy Table of Contents, unless you can be patient.

What kind of ending do you want? What will it look like? What impression will you leave the readers with when they close the book?

How do you want the protagonist to end up? In what physical / intellectual / emotional state?

How does the P react when s/he has the dear desire in hand?

How will the reader know that the P has triumphed? (Even in a series, the P has to triumph at the end of each novel. Why else does a reader keep reading? Because a well-liked P has won once and will need to win again.)

~ Danger, Danger, Danger ~

~~ Plot 3 = What is the protagonist's greatest stress point (at least in the preliminary view)?

How will the protagonist feel at her/his lowest point? What event will put her/him there?

How will s/he recover?

How will the P react in a different manner than the Antagonist to losing? Why would this be the blackest moment in the entire book?

~~ Plot 4 = Antagonist's early triumph over the Protagonist.

The antagonist has seemingly won, either in preventing the P from achieving the dear desire or in simply blocking the P from a major step on that journey to achieve it. What occurred?

How does the P react?

How does the A?

Where will each go from here?

~~ Plot 5 = Final Battle.

This is not the ending, Plot 2. This is the moment the protagonist takes the antagonist *down*! Fist pump!

What sets up the final encounter between the protagonist and the antagonist?

How is this the ultimate encounter? Set the stakes high: this is the defeat of the representative of evil by the representative of honor. Life and death, whether the death is bloody and absolute cessation of life or merely the complete loss of reputation and standing, the death struggle will be the ending of all conflict between the P and the A.

What special skill or learning will the P have that allows her/him to defeat the A? Make a note of where that skill / learning will be acquired during the course of the story. Make another note of proving the P has learned the skill, even if that skill is shakily performed.

What will the P and the A do at the end of the final battle?

~ Two Planned Ironies ~

~~ Plot 6 = Early Twist

What the Protagonist expects that will NOT occur.

You are working with early irony here. The protagonist needs to expect an event that will be helpful to her/him. What is the expectation that the protagonist wants to exult over?

What or who will prevent this early event from occurring? Do not confuse this event with the Antagonist's Early Triumph. While you will answer the same questions, the event will be a completely different scenario.

If you already have other twists in mind, go ahead and write those.

~~ Plot 7 = Seeming Ally's betrayal.

Betrayal is one of those things that hits everyone in the gut.

This is another scenario presenting irony, usually occurring before the Protagonist's Greatest Stress Point (and often setting it up) or occurring before the Final Battle.

The purpose of the SAlly's Betrayal is to show the P's ability to keep pursuing the dear desire, even in the face of betrayal.

Study the meaning of the word "betrayal". It is not disloyalty. Or broken promises. Or simple infidelity or unfaithfulness. It is treachery. It is as deep as a heart stabbed from behind when the P expected a hug.

Of the 7, this may be the most important scene. Don't skimp on it.

A Master Book of the Book

Based on the plot structure chosen, the Master Book of the book helps writers control the story as it turns into a massive maelstrom. The writer has to control the chaos, or the chaos will control the writer.

In the Master Book, each scene in each chapter needs a two-sentence summary. Write one to two sentences about situations and locations in each chapter.

As you write each chapter, make a note of tidbits needed for continuity: Where did people go? To see who? Do what? It can be difficult to keep track of all that. The Master Book is a life-saver for this.

Note down any special twists you have planned. It helps you remember them.

Also helpful are images or a collage or word-pictures about settings and things in your settings. I always draw a house plan. Some writers who have sprawling worlds draw maps to keep track of the location of various scenes.

Develop 7 Work Steps

These 7 Work Steps are the ones that will build a strong foundation for your story and then for your book.

~ 1st: Rough Draft ~

No tinkering, no editing, just writing.

Take the Plot 7 and write the described scenes and all intervening sequels. Launch into that book. About 40 pages in, you will realize if you have a working story or not.

That note you made about a special skill / learning: where does it go in the course of your story? What needs to happen? Who needs to help the protagonist achieve that skill / learning? Where does that character come into the story (more than once, please)?

What other special skills / learning need to occur to set up escape from the Greatest Stress Point?

What foreshadowing about the SAlly's betrayal needs to occur?

If the story just won't launch, set it aside and start another one. The time for Project 1 may not be now. Try Project 2. Try Project 3. Don't try Project 4. Go back and try to determine what was wrong with 1 or 2 or 3.

~ 2nd, Finish ~

Finishing is key. The story doesn't breathe until you finish. Stick with a project until its conclusion. You can have other projects in the opening and ending stages, but you should only be drafting and revising one project at a time.

Many, many wannabe writers have dozens of stories, but they haven't finished one of them. Drafting a book is exceptionally difficult and very important. Many wannabes abandon the draft, or they keep writing and re-writing the beginning or favorite scenes.

Finishing a book teaches that we can push through the hard scenes and sequels. Once we have the draft finished, a new mindset of revision takes over. After that comes proofing, a third mindset. And a writer needs familiarity with all three.

~ 3rd: Add to the Draft ~

This is the revision step. Additions enrich the story and present your voice.

Add in descriptions of characters and settings. Expand on events. Provide the viewpoint character's thoughts and feelings during scenes. P.S. Some people can do the added information as they write the rough draft. I can't. I need a separate step. (I *know!* I *wish!*)

~ 4th: Discover Plot Holes ~

Finding plot holes can only be done by re-reading the whole manuscript, hopefully in one day. Make notes about problems and where to add more hidden clues. Then add them.

And read the whole thing again.

~ 5th: Keep Characters on Firm Ground ~

In your read through, you may discover character discrepancies. Every character's personality should be set from the beginning, even the SAlly's personality. Check actions and reactions to ensure consistency.

A character who changes mid-book or book-to-book is extremely irritating to the reader. Don't irritate your readers. Woo them.

~ 6th: Foreshadow Sly Evil ~

Add in early examples of the antagonist's villainy or outright evil.

The A's minions need to show up as bad people. They can avoid evil, but they definitely need to be people who have chosen the wrong path.

Ensure that your SAlly has three touches that hint at her/his true character allegiance to something other than the Protagonist (whether or not that allegiance is to the antagonist) or merely to the self.

~ 7th: Enhance your Writing ~

Every fifth manuscript page or so, work in an example of figurative language or a special sentence structure. These touches will make you the writer stand out.

Figurative language includes but is not limited to simile, metaphor, personification, and symbolism (color symbolism is easy to work in). An implied metaphor can be a simple as "life is a road with its many junctions and curves and hills".

Special sentence structures include antithesis (juxtaposition / war and peace), chiasmus (a personal favorite / plan the work and work the plan), alliteration (easy to exhibit / dusty death), asyndetons / polysyndetons, zeugmas, anaphoras / epistrophes, and auxesis (often called climactic structure). Most people haven't learned about sentence structures beyond declarative / imperative / interrogatory / exclamatory. Nevertheless, they recognize them and enjoy their occurrence.

Here's a quick easy website for examples and explanations of each. These are sometimes called schema or rhetorical devices: **web.cn.edu/kwheeler/schemes.html** provides easy glances while **rhetoric.byu.edu/** is more complex.

Don't overload the MS page with these enhancements. That's injecting yourself into the story which can be jarring to the reader. (The reader will think, *Oh, yeah, we got an artsy-fartsy author who thinks highly of herself. Not certain I like that.*)

Some writers are known for their lyricism: Robin McKinley comes to mind. Cormac McCarthy. Mary Stewart. They are few in number. If you are a poet at heart, keep the poetry to every fifth MS page until you get a following of readers.

An Official Deadline Creator for Newbie Writers: NaNoWriMo

For newbies, NaNoWriMo is the National Novel Writing Month. This is the internationally infamous writing challenge to churn out 50,000 words in a month, and writers do it with deadlines.

Fifty thousand. 50,000. That's about 1,667 words a day.

That doesn't sound like a lot. Trust me; it is. Do the math. A well-constructed five-paragraph essay (Remember those?) is about 500 words. The 1,667 NaNoWriMo daily goal is more than three times that.

So, the daily goal is three great five-paragraph essays. Most students take 1 ½ hours to write one essay. The daily goal is then 4 ½ hours per day, carcass in chair, writing without looking up.

The month-long challenge is a primo opportunity for a newbie to start the journey to professional writer. NaNoWriMo teaches the newbie the very important discipline needed to create a new life for ourselves, a writing life.

With NaNoWriMo, writers can stop thinking of writing as a hobby and resolve to turn it into a profession, to create a New Advent.

Consider the month like an internship or the probationary term for a new job. It is an intensive apprenticeship. Not only does it teach the work discipline, but the program provides through guiding materials and support groups the kind of helps that any apprentice or intern would receive at a job-site.

~ Who Needs to Participate ~

The challenge provides a great exercise for all writers. We should participate at least once in our writing life. If we feel burned out, the white-hot drive of creativity will recharge us—after it drains us. For the total newbies, NaNoWriMo forces us to work past what we think is our stopping point and teaches us how to do that.

This opportunity is especially helpful to writers stuck between hobby and job. It's not limited to fiction; non-fiction writers like bloggers can also benefit. Through constant deadlines that we must push to achieve, we learn self-discipline.

~ Where to Start? ~

For NaNoWriMo, before the start of November, you can develop your Three 7's (above) or just consider these 4 areas.

Characters :: get to know the primaries. How are they going to collide? Check out Chapter 4 for a slightly different take on character types/

Situation :: understand the remote and near causes *and* effects of major events.

Plot :: How will you pace the story? Many writers talk about scenes and segues or the III-Act structure. Basically, you should know the start and the end and 5 twists between (Plot 7 or chapter 3).

Research :: Special settings. Special elements (steam machines, zeppelins, etc.). Know how the things work.

If you haven't done any of this by the time NaNoWriMo starts on November

1, even if you don't have a story prepped, just start writing and go. As scenes develop, put them where they need to be in the sequence. This sounds like the free-est possibility of all.[13]

Do sit down and figure out where you want all this writing to go. Make yourself have a deadline of the Plot 7 by the tenth of the month.

~ What to Do? ~

As you write, create a master book about your book. (Even a blog series is actually a book.) In your master book, put certain things about your characters and plot or blog sequence or the logical headings for non-fiction topics. Work chapter by chapter, scene by scene within each chapter.

~When to Resort to Tools ~

Computer or pencil/paper doesn't matter, whatever tool you are most comfortable with is the one you use. The computer will keep track of your word count, which you will need to turn in to NaNoWriMo by following consistent deadlines.

Some writers enjoy *Scrivener*, a relatively inexpensive software that can be purchased from Literature and Latte. I've heard of other writer-focused software: Storyshop and the like. Not for me. I don't turn on my laptop every day. Out of my sight is often out of my mind. Others work extremely well on computer software.

You can take the inexpensive cost of the software and buy something to keep in front of you. A science project board or a long board used in art. On both boards, you can use index cards (4 x 6) to write those summary sentences about situation and locations in each chapter.

I use a foam board. I map out plot points on cards. After I finish a rough draft of a chapter, I thumbtack it to the board at the appropriate plot point. Seeing my book building itself is a great incentive. And it's out where I can see it, think about it, and not forget about it.

Tools for character discovery :: online templates or print-outs written by hand. I can't stress primary character discovery enough. No one wants to be one-third of the way into the novel and realize the main character is still a stranger whose basic personality keeps changing. We've read books like that:

---

[13] The two types of writers are Pantsters (writing by the "seat of their pants") and Plotters (writing after planning). Most people are a combination of the two. Professional writers switch it up, but they usually are a conglomeration of the two. And yes, the word "conglomeration" was a deliberate choice.

frustrating!

~ Why to Abandon Tools ~

Do NOT search hours for different things to throw into your book. Do NOT scan through PINterest looking for the perfect plot chart or character breakdown, the 7 best villains or the 5 most romantic locations for a break-up. Don't. This month is not the time for searching and looking.

This is the month to write and keep writing. This is the month to set deadlines and achieve them! Toss procrastination into the waste bin.

Boring? Rewrite later. Too slow? Rewrite later.

Too fast? Do look at this one. Pick the pieces to break the long scene into. Construct the new scenes. Write those.

Don't know if it's good enough? Judge later. Write now.

Basically, keep writing until you reach the end[14]. How do you know it's the end? You'll be satisfied.

The satisfaction won't last long, so savor that brief moment. After NaNoWriMo is over, more work awaits. This is where a lot of newbie and wannabe writers quit. Don't be one of them.

Gut. Fix plot holes and character discrepancies. Add and revise. Improve and enhance and build.

Add similes and metaphors, symbols and sentence structures. Elaborate on dialogue and descriptions. Work in hidden clues. Sharpen the red herrings so they flash.

Divide and conquer. Re-consider and twist. Make people devious. Make readers angsty.

~ How to Succeed ~

50,000 words in 30 days is hard. How do we succeed? Simple: don't try for perfection. Try to finish. Actually, don't try. Just do it. Finish it.

Chuck Windig tells us, "In 2009, NaNo had 167,150 participants, and 32,178 'winners'. That's a pretty good rate, just shy of 20% completion. The numbers

---

[14] For NaNoWriMo, no satisfaction is allowed until after 50,000 words. Throwing hands up in frustration is not satisfaction. Walking away because it's too hard is not satisfaction. Abandonment of the project or flipping from one project to another is not allowed. Be a Pro. Stick with it until it's finished.

get a bit more telling when you look at the number of published novels that have come out of the entire ten-year program, and that number appears to be below 200 books. Out of the 500,000 or so total participants of NaNo over the years, that's a very minor 0.04%."

Read his blog at Terrible Minds, "25 Things you should know about NaNoWriMo ". Not only will it make you snort, you'll laugh, too.[15]

Of the people who take the challenge of NaNoWriMo, barely 20 % finish. I would guarantee the statistics become more sobering when we think of everyone who says, "I'm going to write a book" but never takes it to completion. Less than half of Windig's 0.04% for published manuscripts would be a safe bet to make.

But we're going to be risky. We're going to do NaNoWriMo.

We're going to learn to set deadlines and achieve them!

By accepting the NaNoWriMo challenge and achieving consistent deadlines, we are changing who we are as writers.

Wrapping Up

Working to a deadline is only the first change in our thinking necessary for our transformation from hobby writer to professional writer. (Actually, these lessons apply for any hobbyist who wants to become a professional. They apply for any newbie at the debut of a career. They apply for anyone launching after a season of drifting.)

Deadlines are KEY. Ignore deadlines, and watch the dream fritter away, flutter-by, flutter bye-bye.

Deadlines save us when we approach our first challenge. Yet more challenges remain. As for now, get to writing. 1,667 words a day. **Follow along. Consider. Transform.**

---

[15] http://terribleminds.com/ramble/2011/10/04/25-things-you-should-know-about-nanowrimo/

Chapter 2 ~ One Latin Phrase :: Nulla Dies Sine Linea.

No days without lines.

It would take "nulla dies sine linea" to write the massive *War and Peace,* wouldn't it? Leo Tolstoy used it. As many revisions as that tome faced (and his wife Sofia handwrote every revision, sometimes up to 30: wonderful woman), Tolstoy needed that Latin phrase.

This little phrase is key.

And it is extremely hard to do. Life interferes so easily.

Yet we need to make this our mantra: *Nulla dies sine linea. Nulla dies sine linea. Nulla dies sine linea.* And then we must follow-thru with the action of those words.

According to the Roman historian Pliny, a painter named Apelles originally coined the phrase. Anthony Trollope shares it as his mantra in his *Autobiography.*

Nulla Dies Sine Linea.

It works.

It works even if you are only generating two or three pages a day. Even if you can only manage one page a day. It's the cumulative effect that matters.

We must WRITE EVERYDAY.

That needs to be a shout. We don't need to accept any excuses.

This is a profession. Treat it like one. We go to the 9-to-5 grind every day. Therefore, we need to write every day. *Nulla dies sine linea.*

Look, we have to treat writing like the job it is. It's not our hobby. We let other people think it's our hobby. After all, we're at home.

Look at the ways we let them interrupt us:

- They say, "You can watch the kids for a little while." But that's the little while that we worked all week to get to.
- When we refuse to go on an outing, like the movies or shopping, they say, "How selfish you've become. You don't even want to go out with family and friends."
- They say, "We can sit and talk and watch TV together. I mean, you're not doing anything anyway, are you?"

No other profession is so easily interrupted and so hard to pick back up after interruption.

We must guard our little snippets of time. We carved them out; we must use them. *Nulla dies sine Linea.*

Some writers—the ones who've made **$$$$**—rent office space. They "go" to their offices to write. If they didn't, all the little tugs on their sleeves, just for this little bit, will mean that they get nothing accomplished. Some writers work early in the morning. Before the family climbs out of bed, they can pursue an hour or two of good, fresh word spillage.

Nulla dies sine linea. Put pen to paper.

Having the smallest daily flow of creative energy fires up even more creative energy. Choke it, stifle it—and our world darkens.

As Anais Nin said,

> *We write to expand our world when we feel strangled, or constricted, or lonely. We write as the birds sing, as the primitives dance their rituals. If you do not breathe through writing, if you do not cry out in writing, or sing in writing, then don't write, because our culture has no use for it. When I don't write, I feel my world shrinking. I feel I am in a prison. I feel I lose my fire and my color.*[16]

Nulla dies sine linea.

Surely we can carve out some time.

We do want massive blocks of time, yet few people get what they want. An

---

[16] From her *In Favor of the Sensitive Man, and Other Essays*, published in 1976.

hour here, 30 minutes there, 15 here. Our goal is to have every increment count, no matter how small (as Horton discovered, when he heard a Who.)

Plan to Write / Write to the Plan

The lesson of chapter 1, Deadlines, is just as important when we begin working with our plan. We have the amount of writing we want to accomplish; we have the time we need to spend. Now we need to use it.

Deadlines help us reach our goals.

We plan our goal: brownies, racing, church service. Then we listen for the ding of the oven that lets us know the brownies are ready. Or we look for the checkered flag at the finish line of the Brickyard 500. We bow our heads for the benediction at the end of a service, when some people have their hearts already out the door.

We aim for the deadlines and drive and drive until the end.

Our reward, beside chocolatey goodness, is the completed project in our hands along with the knowledge that we can send that project into the world. All that measuring, all that stirring, all that waiting, and we have fudgy, gooey brownies to drink with our afternoon coffee.

In chapter 1 is the work process needed to turn ideas into a completed manuscript, starting with the original prep of character and plot development.

However, that work process can be a long slog through mucky mire, with red clods sticking to our shoes and following us everywhere.

So, the deadline is not enough. We have to commit to the deadline.

And re-commit to that deadline every single day.

~ Plan the Work ~

First, we have to know what needs to be done. What story stage have we reached? Still sketching ideas? Still developing characters? Got 50 pages of the draft done? Yippee!

No, wait, don't start revising yet. Don't polish it up. Don't run through a final edit.

Let me introduce you to Robert Heinlein, famous writer of pulp fiction and science fiction. Heinlein wrote a lot. Really, a LOT. He had 5 Rules of Writing, the first two of which are very important for us.

Robert Heinlein's First Rule of Writing relates to our mantra. Heinlein speaks all of his Rules with the sonorous weight of the writer who has struggled and knows what leads to achievement.

Rule # 1: You must write.

Rule # 2: Finish what you start.

In other words, write every day.

Focus your writing on the section of the work that you need to complete. And complete that section before you move on to the next focus.

Yes, yes, we can squeeze in a little work here and there: 15 minutes waiting at the doctor's office, 30 minutes waiting to pick someone up, a blessed hour of silence when the words pour out.

We have to use that time to achieve our goals.

~ Work the Plan~

To have every increment count, we first admit that writing anything is a multi-step process, and we writers are multi-tasking throughout every part of it. Just think of how much story we are juggling in our heads every time we sit down to write a scene?

Sketching:: the white-hot creative flow. A largish block of time is needed.

First step of any project is the creative preliminary look: the Sketch. This is the sparked idea, the one that excites us, the glimmer of the final project that we see shining at the top of the great pyramid.

The final project may not look anything like our glittering wondrous creative spark--or it may. This is the starting point. Let the ideas pour out. Ignore every language rule you ever learned. Ignore spelling and capitalization and sentence structure. Ignore anything that anyone has ever said about writing novels.

And when you sit back with a sigh and say, "Yes. That's it. That's what I want," then this idea is sparked.

This may take an hour or two. Or it might be a sentence in a journal that you come back to later and spend a time exploring.

Get the ideas on paper rather than some electronic device. Be able to hold the idea in your hand. That tangible connection creates a bond with your mind.

Planning:: stop and go, so small increments work. Can be interrupted.

The Plan includes character and plot development. Research for anything special fits here as well; you want that special thing swirling around embryonically generating ideas. You'll need a large block of uninterrupted time, but the parts of the Sketch can be broken into sections.

In other words, don't get fascinated by Protagonist's Greatest Stress Point (plot) when you haven't finished considering your protagonist's personality (character).

Drafting:: some creativity, some grunt work. Can sometimes be easily interrupted, but not always.

The basic bulk of the project in a workable form that presents a view of the finished project: the Draft is the hardest part, no matter what profession you are in.

The Draft will never look perfect (unless you're the genius we all hate and churn about 1,000s of perfect words each day). It has flaws; let it bask in those flaws.

Remember, we're writers. Writers write. And re-write.

The draft, though, is the very thing that most wannabe writers never complete. It's the importance of Heinlein's Rule # 2. It's finished. And once finished, it can be improved.

Much like the Sketch, when you're drafting, don't worry about your English teachers and professors. Ignore them. Toss them out the window. Get that story on paper.

Then print it out. Hug the draft to you. It's your child, birthed by you through much labor. Give it love. Because in just a little bit, you'll have to give it Tough Love.

Revising:: demands creative flow. We need the largest block of time without interruptions. This is where everything becomes better.

Now that your manuscript has had its love, time to give it some discipline.

Revising requires a return to creativity. You are judging the scenes that you have, adding new ones, gutting the useless ones, and enhancing all that stays. You are tweaking descriptions and sequences. You are checking the flow of scenes and sequels.

You are adding little twists of characters. Tucking in clues and foreshadowing.

And you are playing with the language without creating sacred cows that must be sacrificed.

Add it. Correct it. Then read the manuscript as one great gulp to check for more.

Proofing and Editing:: Since this step can be picked up and set down easily, use for the smallest increments of time.

In these two stages of work, you are turning to your old English teachers and professors. Yep, you do have to listen to them. Occasionally. For the basic rules of Standard American English or whatever Standard language form you are using, you need to pay attention to the punctuation coding and spelling and capitalization and sentence structure and paragraphs and dialogue tags.

Your readers certainly will spot your errors.

The story may be powerful enough to hold them through the errors in order to reach the end.

But we need them to come back for the next book.

Proofing requires another re-read through of the manuscript. Turn off the creative side of your brain. Turn on the editor. Be cold. Be logical. Hate the words. Hate the commas and push them where they go.

All so that your readers will love the story as much as you do.

Plan the Work to Work the Plan[17]

If we plan our work, we can work our plan. We become more efficient when we know ways to use every increment, from the large blocks to the smallest segments.

Planning is not a calendar, but a plan needs a calendar.

How is it not a calendar? A plan means that you're working on a project. Break the project into its constituent parts. What makes a book?

~ Different Eyes Looking at the Writing Plan ~

Sketching :: 1] the idea. 2] the theme or tagline > the unexpected element that

---

[17] I first came across this sentence in a Dale Carnegie publication, years upon years ago. My mother handed it to me. I wish I had done more than read the words. I wish I had taken them to heart. Thank you, Mom, belatedly.

sets this work apart from others. This sets the book's or blog's niche. 3] Run a Plot 7. Beginning in 2 steps, End in 2 steps, the Middle 3 steps that takes the writing from Beginning to End. Shuffle into order.

Planning :: 1] Develop your characters. 2] Find your settings and special elements. 3] Connect the Plot 7 to a particular plot method.

Drafting :: Write the book, beginning to end, fitting your draft to the chosen plot method. This will be the hardest job of all. Everything else is easy.

Revising :: A developmental editor will find plot holes and discrepancies, character hiccups. Look at pacing: faster, slower, glossing required. Show, don't tell. Revise again. Third time's charm.

Proofing & Editing :: A line editor will help with word usage, grammar / usage / mechanics, and other ticky little problems that people notice the most.

How do these divisions fit onto a calendar? The calendar won't dictate your writing world until you see the average speed at which you work: number of words per day, number of words needed to finish the book, turned into a math equation.

The calendar's sole purpose is to keep you focused. It notes what you should be doing and what's next and next and next. Use that calendar.

1st, plan this week.

Plan for six days of the week. You should have no more than three projects to work on. The primary project is whatever you are drafting or revising. The secondary project should be something that needs finishing off and which can be interrupted. The third project is something to give your creative brain a little respite from the primary project.

Stay on track through the week. Don't stress if you get behind. Plan a make up or shift to the next week. If you get ahead, don't over-plan for the next week.

Every night, look over the next day's focus. Consider the scene. The brain will work on the plan while you sleep. Yes, your brain will dream your work—creative ideas come from dreams.

On the seventh day, whichever day that you pick for your day off, take the day away from the primary project. Play with writing by doing a creative exercise. This prevents burn-out. Also, on the seventh day, plan the next week. You should be able to look ahead a few days and schedule your writing time and projected word count on your primary project.

2nd, plan the month.

On the last seventh day of the month, look ahead to the next month. Determine your primary project focus. Be realistic. Don't over-extend. Add in required days off. Know the errands that have to be done weekly and monthly (e.g., grocery shopping and bill paying). Schedule time for life.

3rd, plan the season.

As you end each season, look into the next. Seasonal planning keeps you on track and keeps you adjusting, especially in the early days of your writing career. You see how many interruptions are occurring; you see how much work you can accomplish. And you adjust to fit.

Plan a realistic primary project for each quarter of the coming year.

- If you're a fast writer, each season could be a manuscript: four novels a year.
- If you're slow, each season could be a major stage of the book: the prep, the draft, the revision, the proof and cover and marketing.

4th, plan the year.

Write your year's plan where you will see it constantly. What are your three major projects? Marketing and promotions, by the way, should count as a project. Schedule for marketing.

Check things off. Highlight things. Put up sticky notes; take them off and adjust as needed.

Follow the plan and write a small amount every day: *Nulla dies sine linea.*

A Plan Creates Magic

Let's do Math!

Most manuscript pages should follow standard size. That's a letter size page with one-inch margins written in Times New Roman (yes, I know it's ugly) font size 12.

The average number of words on a single page set up for standard is **250**.

250 words x five pages = 1,250. Can you write 5 pages a day for four days a week? That's **5,000** words.

5,000 words over 10 weeks (two months and two weeks) is **50,000** words.

Now, that's a novel. It's not an epic, but it is a novel.

Short stories are under 8,000 words. A novelette is about 8,000 to 18,000 words. A novella runs from 18,000 to 40,000 words. A novel starts at 40,000. It once was a fact that different genres required different lengths. In the day of self-publishing, the hard and fast genre-length mandate is falling apart.

However, we're counting words to determine work habits.

Let's set our number of days working at 1,000 words per day for five days a week? Give yourself a day for the business of writing. Take off one day for rest, creativity, and planning. Keep in mind that emergencies and errands will throw everything off.

1,000 words for five days is 5,000 words (same number of words you can accomplish working a bit longer for four days a week.

Here's more math.

250 x 5 pages = 1,250 x 5 days = 6,250 words a week x 4 weeks (a month) = **25,000** words. And you're not even pushing.

6.250 words a week for 50 weeks of the year (take a one-week vacation and have the other days for relationship commitments and generate **312,500** words or 1,250 pages. Now, that's an epic.

Robert B. Parker, writer of the series with the famous tough guy & poet Spenser, wrote five pages every day but Sunday. In a year that's **1,565 pages or 391,250 words** (at about 250 words per page).

 Admittedly, many of those pages are likely revisions of other pages and some of those pages have to be gutted and re-worked, but STILL! Drips and drips will fill up a bucket.

Word by word, that's how novels (and blogs) are written.

Watch the miracle occur. Wisely using small increments will miraculously generate more work. Even more miraculously, larger increments of time will show up in our busy schedules.

Wrapping Up

In a blog for Chuck Windig's Terrible Minds website, Susan Spann gives "25 Things You Need to Know about Writing Mysteries."[18] Spann is writer of the

Shinobi Mystery series. She says with an all-caps shout, "FIND WHAT WORKS FOR YOU AND **DO IT EVERY DAY**." [I put the bold in ;)]

You commit to the **BOLD** in your writing life and see what happens.

It's simple. It just takes commitment.

Nulla dies sine linea. Write every day.

---

[18]   http://terribleminds.com/ramble/2013/10/15/25-things-you-need-to-know-about-writing-mysteries-by-susan-spann/

Chapter 3 ~ One Guiding Decision :: Plot It

White-hot writing--not worrying about plot or characters, just letting the story flow--now that is fun!

At some point, however, that flashover of creativity burns out. We know all those chaotic thoughts need order to turn into a story. That ordered structure, event to event to event, is plot.

As a writer staring at the chaos, a story without form and void, our guiding decision is to select the right plot for our story.

Building Story

Plot is the foundation of all story. ALL story.

The key to any construction job is the foundation. People buy houses based on the square footage they need and the look of the life they want. The buyers don't consider the state of the foundation; that's the job of the builder. And the foundation is buried in the ground, unseen, doing its job without any acclaim or gratitude or blessing. Without a strong foundation, however, the whole structure will fall apart.

So it goes with story. People may love the characters and chatter excitedly about events and the genre tropes, but everything—everything—in that story will fall apart if the foundation is not solid. Should story-tellers neglect plot, the story suffers, and not even the most wonderful characters and stupendous events and twisty tropes can rescue it.

So I say it again: Plot is the foundation of story.

While we writers may begin with a white-hot "what-if" scenario or a character we're burning to explore, we must admit (and admit it *early* in our creative process) that we need a foundation to reveal the hearts and souls of our characters.

Without a solid foundation, no one will buy our house—or our story.

Building Avant Garde

I have a particular love of modern houses and furniture designs. I like non-tradition for its very difference: the new view of exteriors and living spaces, the juxtaposed twist on forms, the clever use of old materials in new ways, the strong shake that modern gives to the idea of home. Yet even Frank Lloyd Wright's Falling Waters depended on a strong foundation.

Experimental poetry like Lawrence Ferlinghetti's "Constantly Risking Absurdity" and e.e.cummings' "but" and David Bottom's "The Sun" may seem edgy and new, *avant garde*. As challenging as they are to read, experimental poems still depend upon certain foundational elements of the poetry genre.

Modern writers, even the absurdists, still manage to use foundations for their texts. Their plays and stories are as much negative mirrors of a type of plot as they are anything. Even though it may seek to avoid, the most *avant garde* text still reveals its foundation.

Tilt your head a little sideways and think metaphor. See it yet? Like a painter manipulating negative space, the image is still revealed.

~ Conundrum One ~

Absence is negative space which is revelatory to the Presence. What's in front of us (presence) may look "gone" (absence), but it still remains, waiting to be seen and understood.

The frustrations that most readers (and viewers) have with some stories and films are their lack of a strong foundation. They never quite reach a destination.

People might claim a love of edgy chaos—but they don't, not really. Just leave a story without its foundational climax and hear the wails. Frank Stockton's "The Lady or the Tiger?", anyone?

~ Conundrum Two ~

The role of any writing is to communicate. If you're not communicating, are you writing? Or scrambling?

Avant garde literature may attempt to avoid plot, but a close examination reveals the foundation, sometimes a mishmash that leaves no one happy except the artist who thinks s/he's "modern".

Let me dispel a couple of myths. First, nothing is new. *Avant garde* is not even new. And should such works somehow endure for centuries, they are merely studied as the oddities that they are while writers like Shakespeare continue to entertain and enlighten us.

Take the most modern work we can find, apply a basic plot type, and we discover much. Once we see the foundation, we discover that it's not as new and edgy as we originally thought.

Writers who cry, "My story's different; my story's new; my story's unique" can expect this shock: it's not. I do regret offending you, but truth has thorns. In all the millennia that people have told stories, all the possible combinations have already occurred. Nothing's new under the sun.[19]

Building Plot: Booker's 7 Types of Plot

When I first encountered this information—without any context—I assumed the Booker Prize People presented it.[20] I was wrong, very, very *wrong*.

In his 2004 book *The Seven Basic Plots: Why We Tell Stories* (influenced by Carl Jung), Christopher Booker[21] returns to the roots of story.

No matter what kind of fiction you write (and this works for even much of the nonfiction realm), the foundational structure will fit one of these 7 Types. Booker has staked a powerful claim. How can it be, that for all the stories in the world, from the most ancient myth to the most disaffected absurdist modern, only seven basic plots exist?

If that claim is true, it will work across all times and all genres. Let's try it.

---

[19] Ecclesiastes 1:9

[20] We know what happens when people assume. I also should have known better, but I was crediting them with more sense.

[21] People have taken me to task about even looking sideways at Christopher Booker. Among other crimes, he's very old-fashioned views about women's places in society. So did my grandfathers. Time changes. Some people change with the enlightenment that comes with time. Some don't. In Chapter 5 I do have a discussion about those people who don't want to change. The point? I'm not going to ignore Booker's literary insights just because I don't agree with his social commentary.

Overcoming the Monster: *Beowulf, Jaws, Lord of the Flies, King Lear, Alien, Pride and Prejudice, Fried Green Tomatoes, Atonement*

Rags to Riches: *Cinderella, Aladdin, Oliver Twist, Great Gatsby, Prince and the Pauper, Good Deeds, Pretty Woman*

The Quest: *Watership Down, Raising Arizona, Willow, Raiders of the Lost Ark, Avatar, The Best Exotic Marigold Hotel, Northanger Abbey*

Comedy: anything by Aristophanes, anything by the Marx Brothers, *Airplane, The Blues Brothers, Animal House, A Walk in the Woods, Arsenic and Old Lace, Bringing Up Baby, Much Ado about Nothing, A Midsummer Night's Dream*

Tragedy: *Oedipus, Macbeth, Rebel without a Cause, Frances, Philadelphia, Cool Hand Luke, Bonnie and Clyde, Whatever Happened to Baby Jane?*

Rebirth: *Sleeping Beauty, Beauty and the Beast, A Christmas Carol, Now Voyager, Summertime, Avatar, Persuasion, Under the Tuscan Sun*

Voyage and Return: *Peter Rabbit, The Hobbit, Odyssey, The Lion the Witch and the Wardrobe, Brideshead Revisited, Mansfield Park, Great Expectations, The Tempest*

Whaddya know? Christopher Booker is right. Whether concrete or abstract, real or metaphorical, all sorts of stories do fit these seven categories.

A Detailed Look at the 7 Plot Types

While many plot structures abound (and several are discussed later in this chapter), it is the 7 Plot Types that will give the key that every writer needs to unlock story. The point to that key is coming, I promise, but first let's look at the three required elements for each Plot Type.

In nonfiction, the plot may look more like the outline of an essay. Most nonfiction writing is explaining / informing or persuading / arguing. Yet Booker's 7 Types of plot work equally well as a guide for the informing / persuading writer.

The famed *Who Moved my Cheese?* by Spencer Johnson is actually Overcoming the Monster.

Dave Ramsey's *Financial Peace* is classic Rags to Riches.

Flow: The Psychology of Optimal Experience by Mihaly Csikszentmihali is

The Quest.

The influential *Seven Habits of Highly Influential People* (Stephen Covey) teaches a basic reformation of thought: Rebirth.

On and on, when we look at nonfiction, we see that Booker's 7 Types are also guiding decisions that focus the text.

Think like a Pro could be cast as Rebirth or Overcoming the Monster, but I have focused it as the Quest. Elements of the other types do come into play, just as any informative writing includes elements of the argument, of description, and of narration (the so-called four modes of writing).

Let's examine fourteen works in skeletal form through the 7 Types of Plot in order to determine the three required elements demanded of each.

Overcoming the Monster

This category is not as simple as it seems. We often have difficulty overcoming monsters in our lives. The monsters are not as easily identified as they are in movies.

We must identify the scaring and scarring evil with blood-stained claws. Be it a vampire or merely a life-sucking job, a philandering spouse or an oppressive dictator, all are monsters who destroy other lives. The invidious monsters are the ones who seem friendly, the ones who seem to help our protagonist, the ones who would never, not in a million years, do anything to hurt anyone.

To write more than basic genre, have your protagonist **struggle to identify the real monster**. (1)

We have to **acquire the tools needed to defeat the monster**. (2) Buffy had a training schedule to become a vampire-slayer; our protagonist must train as well. If that monster is a life-sucking boss, how can the protagonist re-set the boundaries between job and life? How will the philandering spouse be discovered? What will enlighten the protagonist to the invidious monsters who present themselves as friends? How will the now-aware protagonist develop the skills necessary to step up and stand against the seemingly-innocent monster?

The actual battle often requires **the sacrifice of something dear**, with no guarantee that anything will ever replace our sacrifice. (3)

Jaws (Peter Benchley)

No believed that a monster shark was terrorizing Amity Island. (1) The protagonist didn't have the skills to locate and fight the monster. Needed to defeat the monster was not just an academic but also a battered seaman: neither would have succeeded without the persistently determined protagonist. (2) The seaman even sacrificed his life in the struggle; the academic nearly did; the protagonist would have without the academic's miraculous return. (3)

Atonement (Ian McEwan)

First, who is the protagonist in the novel? The young girl, not the older sister. She identified the wrong monster—which is not revealed for many years. (1) Her misidentification sends the sister's love interest to prison and destroys the relationship between the sisters. Discovering the true monster (the pedophile who marries his victim) takes years. (2) The tragedy of this novel is not just the doomed love; it continues to the end of the protagonist's life as she admits that she will never get atonement for her early mistake. (3)

Rags to Riches

In badly-written rags-to-riches stories, logic is tossed out as writers drag their protagonists into the luxurious wealth that they think is deserved. In well-written stories, the protagonist is shown developing the skills necessary to gain wealth and succeed in that new environment.

Logic tells us that no one receives something (great) for nothing.[22] The impoverished state needs to be presented along with the dream of greatness that the protagonist has. That **dream should be possible, not improbable**. (1)

The **steps from rags to riches are presented**. (2) What will each step entail? Who/what is essential to gaining the skills that are the part of each step? Who/what will block the step?

The **wealth needs to be reasonable**. (3) Not everyone is descended from royalty or nobility, you know. Some of us were dirt farmers eager to escape our serfdom. (Welcome to America!) Not everyone will walk into a top editor position just because of an association with a mysterious billionaire.

By the way, what is wealth? Money? Or time? Or knowledge? Or relationships? If no money is ever obtained but relationships are deepened, is that an example of the best riches in the world? (Preaching. Sorry. Not.)

Cinderella (the classic fairy tale)

In rags, scrubbing the sooty hearth, but she once was the privileged daughter of a wealthy nobleman. (See, she already comes with a knowledge of the etiquette and behavior necessary for a life as a queen.) She was cast into her

---

[22] If you think that, I have a bridge in Brooklyn that I'd like to sell you.

impoverished position by her father's death and her stepmother's evil.(1) Her stepmother and stepsisters seemingly conspire to prevent her return to her former status if she wins the prince's lottery (random pick, you know.)

Thankfully, she has helpful birds and mice and an extremely helpful fairy godmother who wants to restore balance to this little community. And don't forget the pumpkin! (2) While her path still has problems, she does manage to return to the life into which she was born (see, that's logical.) (3)

Good Deeds (Tyler Perry)

Our protagonist Wesley Deeds has been the good son, running his deceased father's successful family business while his brother acts the prodigal. He dreams of pursuing his own dreams, but he feels bound by his obligations. Wesley is blocked by his fiancée, his mother, and his brother as well as his own sense of responsibility. (1) He has an impoverished life barren of what he needs.

In an interesting juxtaposition, an impoverished single mother begins to enlighten him to the pursuit of what's most important: 1st, in recognizing what a true relationship should be; 2nd, in recognizing that living life is not merely existing. (2)

Reaching for what he wants becomes the pivotal step to a richness of life that he never expected. While the story of the impoverished single mother provides the literal "rags to riches", it's Wesley Deeds who has the greater "rags to riches" rise as he rebuilds from the tatters of his life. (3)

The Quest

Searching for a treasure (tangible or intangible) requires a long journey to distant places in order to achieve a goal—whether that is a physical journey encountering exotic people for material treasure or an intellectual journey encountering exotic ideas for spiritual treasure. Thus, the three elements require ~

Remove the protagonist from the settled, day-to-day existence is the first required step. (1) Thus, the writer must present that mundane existence, showing the protagonist's contrasting satisfaction and dissatisfaction. An impelling event must drive the protagonist into the quest. What is the protagonist's quest? What makes the treasure so necessary to be obtained? The protagonist will be uncomfortable and awkward as s/he launches into the quest; however, the dissatisfaction is strong enough to remaining in the status quo is not an option.

Exhibit the entrance to the place completely new. (2) Know your story's definition of exotic. How is this new place exotic / different from what the protagonist has known before? How are the people in this new place also part of the exotic experience for the protagonist? What is charming about the exotic experience? What remains unsatisfactory, preventing the new place from becoming a paradise?

Discovery of the treasure is like an epiphany. (3) Whether it's the pot at the end of the rainbow that the protagonist finds and uses to improve life back home or the discovery of something richer than was ever anticipated, how is that treasure discovered? Is it at first mistakenly avoided or ignored? If so, what brings the protagonist's attention back to it? How is the treasure a great richness? Does the treasure create such a temptation that return to the ordinary world is no longer a requirement?

Northanger Abbey (Jane Austen)

Our protagonist loves her family and life there, but she wants to experience a daring and racy world. A trip to Bath offers her the opportunity to experience the ton's social whirl and a dash of romance from two different suitors along with a spark or two of danger. (1)

The invitation to Northanger Abbey provides her with a suitably mysterious atmosphere—that she mistakenly tries to turn into a dark mystery. The suitor that she cares about is deeply disappointed by her childish imaginings. (2) When she is banished, she rises to an adult's responsibility and recognition of her mistakes.

Her reward comes when her beloved suitor tracks her down, giving her the sacrifice that true love will willingly make in order to achieve the treasure it most wants. (This change—marriage to her beloved, the treasure that the protagonist wanted—prevents *Northanger Abbey* from being a plot of Voyage and Return.) (3)

The Best Exotic Marigold Hotel (Deborah Moggach)

Recently widowed, our protagonist is left in financial straits with a life constraining life that will only stifle her. She decides to take the little money that she has, seek a new life where she can be independent, and her few skills might provide her more opportunities, and travels to India. (1)

There, she discovers a world that presents difficulties but people who are charming, struggles with certain necessary adaptations but makes meaningful connections. (2) Not only does she find a job for which she is particularly suited, but she has an opportunity for love with a man who is willing to grow in a relationship with her (rather than the closed-off marriage that she had realized she had had with her late husband). (3)

Voyage and Return

This plot category seems very similar to the Quest, except the goal is the return back to the original existence, wiser through the experienced trials and ordeals of the journey.

Normal existence for the protagonist must be presented as exactly what is wanted. (1) The reason for the journey should be dire: destruction of that existence is threatened. (*Identity Thief*'s character portrayed by Jason Bateman is the perfect example.)

The voyage itself may not be "exotic"; it may even seem ordinary on the surface, but it is enriching. (2) It may simply be getting back home, older but not necessarily wiser. Many different kinds of events will occur on this voyage. Great internal transformation will not occur. The goal of this voyage is not a treasure; the goal may not even be specified. If it is specified, then the goal will have much to do with returning home.

Returning home may have obstacles, as events and people may have conspired to work against the protagonist's easy settling back into the life that s/he loves. (3) Thus, the return may be the point of greatest difficulty for the protagonist. However, when all problems are overcome, the life that was threatened is restored, and the sun shines once again on the protagonist and what s/he holds most dear.

Odyssey (Homer)

This ancient Greek epic is the classic example of Voyage and Return. Odyssey so enjoyed his home life that he pretended insanity to avoid participating in the Trojan War. (1) However, when he is discovered (by his little son being placed in danger because of his pretense), he agrees to honor his former vow and travels far from Ithaca to Troy. The Odyssey presents his voyage home.

Among the things that delay his return are his stupid offense to the gods, more than one encounter with monsters, people who create problems, lovely distractions, and outright imprisonment. (2)

Even when he reaches home, he's not home, for outsiders are trying to take his place and no one recognizes him. Thank god he's clever, for he figures out a way to re-introduce him to his son, now 21 years old, discover who his loyal servants are, defeat the invading outsiders, and determine if his wife still loves him after two decades away. (3)

The Hobbit (J.R.R. Tolkien)

Bilbo Baggins doesn't really want to go on a dangerous adventure with complete strangers (and dwarves, of all people!), but he finds himself lured in by Gandalf the wizard. (1)

There's a lot of walking. There's a lot of hiding. There's a lot of arguing. He encounters trolls and elves, goblins and Golem, riddles and rock giants, and a dragon with fire and the dragon of gold. (2)

He returns home, experienced but not really wiser, eager for his own cooking and his own hearth. (3) Oh, and a dangerous ring. But that's another story.

Comedy

In writing story, we distinguish between humor and comedy.[23] Humor is telling jokes. Comedy is the protagonist achieving his goal. I fought the mis-definition of comedy in my classroom; Booker does so with more authority. It seems simple enough to write comedy. However, I will note that in comedy, pathos (deeply emotional moments) occur quite a good bit (while tragedies are often filled with humor).

The protagonist confronts adversity. (1)

That adversity is deepened through a series of confusing events. (2)

The climax clears up all confusion and grants the protagonist the original goal which has transformed in an unexpected way. (3)

To understand more about comedy, look at the information on tragedies and go in the opposite direction.

A Midsummer Night's Dream (William Shakespeare)

Two young ladies are in love with two young men. One young man returns the affection, but her father is an obstacle. One young man does not return the affection. Acceptable as a suitor by the other young lady's father, he's after the money and status that marriage to her would bring. (We won't talk about Theseus' problems with Hippolyta, Oberon's problems with Titania, and Titania's problem with Bottom, okay—although they do add to the confusion.) (1)

A Midsummer Night in the woods, with interference by Puck and fairies, causes all four to fall out of love and into love at cross-purposes. We have

---

[23] Hollywood doesn't, but Hollywood's not about story; it's about making money using the lowest common denominator possible [usually ridicule, usually raunchiness, usually violence, always sex]. Hollywood says that comedy is a show with lots of laugh. Nope. Just nope.

funny lines and funny altercations. (2)

The morning finds them returned to their wits. The first couple remain in love; the second couple are now in love. All is worked out to everyone's (including the father's) satisfaction. (3)

A Walk in the Woods (Bill Bryson) nonfiction

Tasked with walking the Appalachian Trail, Bryson enlists the help of a buddy he hasn't seen in years. Both of them out of shape, they start walking the 2100-mile trail, beginning in Georgia. (1)

Along the way they meet many different adventurers, some who are fellow hikers, some who merely live near the trail but never think about it. Bryson shares the difficulties of hiking over the mountainous terrain in all sorts of weather over such an extended length of time. Eventually, he begins looking for a method to alter his original goal: hop, skip, jump. (2) He reaches the end, Mt. Katahdin in Maine.

In reading, we the readers are treated to Bryson's humor and unique perspective. (3)

Tragedy

In Comedy, all is achieved; in tragedy, all is futile. While death is not a requirement of tragedy, doom is. Writers of tragedy, to prevent unrelenting darkness, will often fill a tragedy with humor. Shakespeare is a master of keeping the audience engaged in the tragic form: *Romeo and Juliet* and *Macbeth* have several laugh-out loud moments that relieve the ratcheting suspense.

The protagonist—through his own actions—**causes his own destruction**. (1) An inner flaw (consider one of the Seven Deadly Sins[24] when constructing a story) sets in motion a domino effect.

While all may seem confused to the protagonist, we can see the steps that bring him to doom. At some point, usually toward the plot's center, the **protagonist takes an irrevocable step**. (2)

The protagonist may see the doom's approach. If he doesn't believe it, he continues forward without check. Most protagonists will act to reverse the approaching doom. How the **protagonist confronts his doom** is equally key: will he run away, or will he lean into it? (3) (in the 1992 *Last of the Mohicans*, the despicable vengeance-focused Magua leans into his doom, his one

---

[24] 7 Deadly Sins: pride, wrath, greed, gluttony, sloth, lust, envy

redeeming moment).

Macbeth (William Shakespeare)

Macbeth wants to be king (pride); the witches prophesy that he will be king; his wife presents a plan to kill the king. This plan will turn his dream into reality. So they kill him—and two innocent guards. (1) And no one says anything, not even Macbeth's best friend Banquo, the only person who might have guessed at Macbeth's secret ambition.

Because Banquo might have suspected Macbeth of killing the former king, Macbeth kills his BFB (2). Now, after Banquo's ghost comes to a banquet, Macbeth's behavior causes questions, and questions lead to rebellion. So Macbeth kills more people, trying to stop the rebellion, but that backfires.

An army marches against him. He meets Macduff (whose family Macbeth had killed), and cries, "Lay on, Macduff, and damned be him who cries 'hold, enough!'" (3) Macduff kills him off-stage and comes back swinging Macbeth's head.

Bonnie and Clyde (story by Robert Benton and David Newman)

Bonnie and Clyde are disaffected misfits who find in each other a love of thrills and violence. They join with another couple, equally disaffected and dissolute.

Content with their corrupted lives, they seek a thrilling and violent way to get money. (1) They rob people, usually small stores and rural gas stations— hardworking people who were merely trying to make ends meet—and murder anyone who corners or confronts them. (2)

As Shakespeare warned in *R & J*—"violent delights lead to violent ends"— they willfully choose violence, they relish that violence, and they are brought to a violent death. (3)

Rebirth

Transformation through reformation. A special branch of the Rebirth story is apotheosis, when the protagonist is transformed into a god. While *Eat, Pray, Love* is often given as an excellent example of a Rebirth plot, I think better examples are *Wild* and *Under the Tuscan Sun*. *Wild* contains a physical and intellectual transformation. *Under the Tuscan Sun* is a three-part reformation of self: the protagonist is no longer intellectually or physically or spiritually the person she was at the beginning.

A mirror is needed. **Some starkly clear representation occurs that awakens the protagonist to "a better life".** (1) The protagonist launches into an attempt to achieve that better life, with flashes of insight and stumbling steps, all of which **teach the protagonist how to change from who s/he is into who s/he wants to become**. (2) Eventually, **a new self emerges**, often in a new place. (3)

Beauty and the Beast (Gabrielle-Suzanne Barbot de Villeneuve)

The Beast terrifies everyone and kills anyone who steals one of his magical roses. When he threatens a merchant, the man promises that his daughter will come and live with Beast. (1) Gradually, her kindness and compassion begin to transform his heart, just as he begins to transform her heart. However, both of them still hesitate, for his physical appearance serves as an obstacle between them.

The curse that originally transformed him can only be broken by true love. (2) An obstacle almost prevents Beauty from telling of her love (In story, interfering families have a lot to answer for.), but she does, given heart because she feared he was dying. He is physically transformed, back into the man he once was, but he is no longer that man, having been intellectually and spiritually transformed by her love. (3)

A Christmas Carol (Charles Dickens)

Miserly Scrooge counts money as more important than people. He barely pays a living wage to his employees, and Dickens paints the Cratchit family in broad strokes designed to evoke our sympathy. (1) Reminders of Scrooge's past coupled with the threat of his future (thank you, dear ghosts) change his heart. (2)

His focus transforms, shifting him away from the accumulation of material gold to accumulating lasting relationships. He becomes compassionate and generous, no longer hated but well-loved because of his benevolence. (3)

The Key to all 7 Plot Types

I promised the key. Anyone who considers writing will need this key. Ready? Here it is, sounding so simple. Stick with the Plot you Pick.

If you pick one of the 7 Types of Plot, use it—and only that one—to guide you from beginning to end.

That sounds too simple, doesn't it? Complexity is needed, isn't it?

Not at the beginning. At the beginning, you need a clear view. Pick one Plot. Post it in front of you every time you sit down to work on that story, and that clear view will keep your developing characters and your exciting events and your selected tropes focused.

People will argue with me and tell you that the story's theme (tagline) is the all-important guide.

Nope. Because of this truth: the TYPE OF PLOT is the first building block to discover the theme. To say it more simply: the theme depends on the plot type. Without the plot type, the theme weakens, characters weaken, and story weakens. And the whole thing will come crashing down. Just like a house with a bad foundation.

Build strong. Set a firm foundation.

Once you have selected from the 7 Types of Plot, you can begin looking at the structure of the whole story. And that leads us to five different plot methods.

Five Methods for Plotting

~ Method 1 ~

Every school unfortunately teaches simplistic plot, otherwise known as Freytag's Pyramid, which can look like a simplistic pyramid. When applied to prose stories, it is merely a simplistic pyramid.

Freytag was presenting the structure of a five-act drama, not prose stories, but his pyramid is taught in language arts classes as if it were gospel. Writers who follow the pyramid quickly encounter difficulties.

The unfortunate truth is that stories are not simple pyramids. For Kurt Vonnegut, his stories go straight down. James Fenimore Cooper writes classic roller coasters.

Imposing Freytag's simplistic plot onto prose fiction twists the point.

However, although it hurts me, here are the five parts of Freytag's Pyramid when used with prose fiction.

Opening (sometimes called exposition). The opening contains the presentation of the characters, central conflict, and major themes.

Rising Action (growing suspense). The term Rising Action does not allow for subplots. Nor does it allow for the protagonist to have rewards as well as setbacks.

Climax (defined as the point of greatest suspense or emotional excitement when it should be defined as the point at which the conflict's end is known). According to simplistic plot, the climax is centered in the story. Unfortunately, because of story analysis, we know that the climax occurs usually at the 80-90% mark in the story's text, not at the 50% mark.

Falling Action. This term implies that a great fall-off of suspense occurs, and it does. However, it doesn't occur for the entire latter part of the story.

Resolution. I have seen high school textbooks define this term as "everything after Falling Action" which is just sad. The resolution should contain the protagonist's revelation or epiphany about the major theme.

~ Method 2 ~

The only writing that could follow a type of pyramid—and please remember that Freytag was discussing the broad structure of drama—is Shakespeare's 5-Act Play Structure.

The 5-Act Play Structure works for his comedies, tragedies, and histories.

Act I = Introduction. Protagonists (who are not first on stage, btw), antagonists, situation, setting, and primary themes and motifs. Shakespeare will open by presenting the situation.

The play opens with a street brawl between the Montagues and Capulets in *Romeo & Juliet.*

The crossed former lovers of Beatrice and Benedict and the new lovers Hero and Claudio are introduced in *Much Ado about Nothing.* The Bs were formerly enamored, but their cutting tongues ruined their love while Hero and Claudio are headed toward marriage.

The ghost of old King Hamlet walks the castle walls at night.

The Archbishop of Canterbury discusses that the new King Henry V is making changes and they discuss plans to keep him from interfering in their traditional world.

The three Weird Sisters swirl around the battlefield as rebels treasonous to the king of Scotland of defeated by the loyal Macbeth.

Act II = Complications. Events occur which deepen the problems for the protagonists.

Romeo declares love to and then marries Juliet. Yes, that's a complication, for Romeo then infuriates Mercutio when he refuses to engage in a duel with his [unknown to anyone] cousin-in-law—which occurs in Act III, and Juliet cannot accept the marriage her parents are forcing her into—which is Act IV.

The mischief-making Don John tries to find a way to cross the love of Hero and Claudio in order to hurt his brother.

Hamlet must find a way to determine if the ghost speaks true about murder. He decides to pretend insanity.

Henry V finds treasoners and takes Harfleur.

Macbeth kills King Duncan, his king and his kin and a guest in his house.

Act III = Crisis. In a tragedy, the protagonist (willingly or unwillingly) takes the fatal step from which there is no return; this step will lead to doom. In a comedy, the protagonist takes a horrible and emotionally-wrought step that would seem to cause great tragedy. History plays follow either the tragic or comedic structure.

Romeo kills Tybalt. This sets up his banishment which causes both he and Juliet to threaten suicide.

Don John sets up Claudio by making him believe Hero is not true, and Claudio rejects Hero at the altar.

Hamlet has enacted the play *The Mousetrap*, which gives him the proof he needs: "the ghost is a true ghost". However, he kills Polonius, which gives Claudius a public reason to get rid of him, causes Ophelia's mental breakdown, and drives Laertes' need for revenge.

Henry V decides to march ahead even though his army is likely to encounter the amassing French forces.

Macbeth sees the ghost of Banquo, the best friend whom he murdered for fear Banquo would suspect that Macbeth had murdered the former king. His very public reaction to the ghost that no one else can see raises questions about his ascent to the throne.

Act IV = Reversal. The protagonist sees doom and works to avert it; the antagonist works to ensure the doom.

Juliet enlists the help of Friar Laurence to avoid what will be a bigamous marriage. Her father moves the marriage up by one day, hastening her drinking of the deathlike-sleep potion.

Benedict challenges Claudio to a duel; Hero is "buried" when she is not dead. Don John's comrades in crime are caught by an inept and ignorant chief watchman. Will the correct information get to Claudio in time?

Hamlet switches the letters to the English king, deliberately causing the deaths of Rosencrantz and Guildenstern. Ophelia drowns. Hamlet has now killed more people than Claudius did.

Henry V defeats the overwhelming army of the French at Agincourt.

Macbeth kills more innocents in his quest to keep the throne.

Act V = Climax and Resolution. Exactly what it says it is.

Juliet awakens as Romeo dies and then kills herself.

The truth is revealed: Hero is true; Don John is evil. All is well.

Hamlet duels Laertes, and each "kill" the other with Laertes' poisoned sword. His mother drinks the poison. Hamlet kills Claudius then dies.

Henry V defeats the French and wins the hand of the French princess Katherine. Through him, their son will inherit the English throne, and through her, their son will inherit the French throne.

The last three prophecies come true, and Macbeth gets his head chopped off by a trunk from Birnam Wood.

The five-act structure is very good for broad sweeps, but writers working with novels need a bit more detail.

~ Method 3 ~

The four-act movement works for many people.

Act the First: Introduce the Trouble. When the trouble starts, the protagonist thinks, "I can solve this problem." His solution is NOT the answer; it makes things worse. This leads to >>

Act the Second: the Doubled Trouble. The fix caused more problems that spread like the flu in unexpected directions. Our protagonist now says, "Okay, this wasn't what I expected or wanted, but I'm good. I can work it out." However >>

Act the Third: the Crisis Point. The Trouble Triples, increasing in physical danger and intellectual suffering and emotional angst. Our protagonist can't go back; retreating will only make the problem worse. Going forward is dangerous but is the only option. "Damned if I do; damned if I don't." His dilemma requires that he abandon—or sacrifice—his first desired goal. He will question his purpose is continuing on.

Act the Fourth: All seems Lost. But the protagonist knows, "I can't give up. I've come too far. There's nobility in dying courageously. I won't give up." So the protagonist takes the necessary and essential and most difficult steps and tumbles into the story's end which is the troubles end. This is the epiphany of love and life.

~ Method 4 ~

Most stories look more like roller coasters than pyramids. The protagonist approaches his goal; an antagonist blocks him. He makes a new drive; another antagonist pushes him. Push only to be rolled back. Much like life—or Sisyphus. Roller-coaster plots are better known as Complex Plots.

Nancy Duarte gave a wonderful TED talk on an organic structure for speeches that is very similar to the roller coaster style of story. This link offers a youtube video: https://www.ted.com/talks/ nancy_ duarte_the_secret_structure_of_great_talks .

She focuses on Martin Luther King Jr. and Steve Jobs, master orators. In a strange way, major speeches are much like story structure, in presenting a goal, a desire with its obstacles that must be overcome. Duarte, interestingly enough, briefly mentions Method 5 (discussed below).

Duarte claims that any communication is the distinction between "what is" (status quo) and "what could be". An organic structure is the best method to help the audience move from complacency with the status quo to motivation for change. By contrasting "what is" with "what could be", master orators create in their audiences a euphoric bliss that motivates their change.

For writers of blogs and speeches or any fiction, Duarte reinforces that Freytag's is too simplistic.

As we work to the conclusion of any communication, Duarte advises us to make the gap between the status quo and the bliss of change as large as possible. For fiction, this means the synergy of the protagonist's push and the antagonist's pull becomes stronger, deeper, and more disparate.

Your terminology for the roller coaster Complex Plot includes~

Narrative Hook is the first moment of suspense, when the reader is hooked into the story. This hook, while intense, does not last long. Consider the opening hook of most James Bond movies: presenting the problem scenario and setting and (often) the antagonist or the minions.

Exposition: see Shakespeare's Act I. It's the same.

Conflict: same again. Once the conflict is clear, the story can move to the next section.

Complications: the bulk of the story, a whopping ¾ of it all. A series of setbacks & achievements in alternating scenes and sequels, with added difficulties as subplots with their own story structures.

Climax: the moment at which the conflict is over.

Resolution (or Denouement): the protagonist's (and the audience's) epiphany about the major theme and the tied-up loose ends for the other elements of the story.

~ Method 5 ~

I don't use any of the above methods ~~ although I have been guilty of teaching three of these methods as if they are gospel.

I use the Archetypal Story Structure as presented by Christopher Vogler in his book *The Writer's Journey*, which builds on Joseph Campbell's Hero's Journey work on the monomyth.

For some reason, this 12-step process clicks in my little brain.

The Ordinary World presents the protagonist in his normal world from which he will be ripped.

The Call to Adventure is the event that will catapult him from the OW complacency into reaching for a new desire.

In the Refusal of the Call, no protagonist should be an idiot. Seeing danger ahead, most protagonists should hesitate—but staying in the OW impossible. J.R.R. Tolkien's *The Hobbit* does this very well: Bilbo doesn't want to go on a great adventure. He's very comfortable in his home. However, the wizard Gandalf says just the right thing to give him the impetus to set out on that journey. Basically, he'll become just like his boring relatives if he doesn't set out on the journey. Bilbo definitely doesn't want that.

Meeting with the Mentor: In order to begin the necessary changes, the protagonist needs a guide. Gandalf is Bilbo's mentor, but the hobbit also finds that the dwarves, consciously and unconsciously, have things to teach him. A chief lesson is about narrow-mindedness: in seeing theirs, he despises his own.

Crossing the First Threshold: Is the protagonist willing to stretch beyond his capabilities and start changing? The encounter with the trolls serves as this step for Bilbo. He must use his wit and his wits to escape their cooking pot.

Tests, Allies, and Enemies is the series of adventures, both set-backs and achievements (think "complications") that continue the protagonist's change from his original complacent self into an individual who confronts personal fears and overcomes them. these events give our protagonist the skills to survive to the end of the story.

The Approach to the Inmost Cave proves the protagonist has changed and is ready to face his greatest fear.

The Ordeal / the Dark Moment requires more (and unexpected) sacrifices from the protagonist. He faces the supreme enemy here: not just overwhelming numbers but also the evil most like himself. In the lair of thousands of goblins, Bilbo encounters Golum. Both are witty, selfish, secretive, and wily. The worst enemies are most like ourselves.

A Reward comes unexpectedly to the protagonist after he escapes the Dark Moment. This reward is better than the world he abandoned and the goal he had to sacrifice before he reached the Dark Moment.

More troubles occur in the Road Back.

Then the evil antagonist returns in the Resurrection, in a worse form (Smaug in *The Hobbit* is a gigantic and fiery Golem in many ways). The protagonist comes closer to death here than at any previous point—and survives.

For the Return with the Elixir, with a new and better goal decided-upon, the protagonist returns to his ordinary world. He is changed, much better than he began.

Pick your plot method wisely.

Deciding on the plot structure that will impose order on the chaos that story can become is the best Guiding Decision you can make.

1st, determine what TYPE of plot will you write; then determine your protagonist's major steps through the story using one of the five methods. (Pick #5! Pick #5!)

Make the Right Decision!

Plot: a Slugfest

Should I or shouldn't I? That's the question for writers.

Should I just launch into writing and see where it takes me? Or should I plot out every scene and sequel, checking all the boxes?

Should I let the ideas flow onto the keyboard, with no idea what I'm thinking or where the story's heading? Turn off old logical and embrace creative inspiration?

Or should I decide which story genre is making the most money then look at the characters that readers chatter about? From that, I can craft a story, step by step, hitting all the tropes and placing my pinchpoints at the appropriate percentage markers in the novel?

Ick. Just ick. For both of them.

~ Why for Which? ~

No discussion of plot is complete unless we also talk about these two diametrically opposed methods of approaching story. Pantsters fly by the seat of their pants. Plotters work everything out beforehand.

There, that's enough, isn't it? I wish.

For pantsters, the mess comes at the end of writing, when they have to make sense of the jumble that poured onto the page. For plotters, the mess comes at the beginning, when they have to make sense of the entire story before they work everything onto the page.

Pantsters do a lot of freewriting and call it chapter development. It's not.

Plotters fill out a lot of templates and call it chapter development. It's not.

The best plot structures re-create a river's flow.

Nothing is a steady current, not even a river in flood. The main stream rushes along until it encounters a boulder or a bend. These obstructions create swirls, eddies, along the banks. The current shifts, dredging deep or gushing freely. The river spews out at its end, like the great overflowing Mississippi whose flood-brown waters pour into the Gulf of Mexico, identifiable miles after the river itself has ended.

This is the reason I despise Freytag's pyramid and design my plots with the Archetypal Story Pattern (or James Scott Bell's *Super Structure* http://www.jamesscottbell.com/styled-7/styled-5/index.html

~ Plot Point? ~

I spent a few years as a pantster. Embarking on a story with little more than a character and an idea is very seductive.

I spent a few years as a plotter. Structuring a story around the plot points sped up the drafting process, and the flailing around for inspirational creativity vanished.

Writers can make money constructing stories, one after another, based on a lock-step pattern. They're easy, quick, safe. Measure in two characters, so very like previous characters, add these tropes with a dash of different spices, bake at 350 for 45 minutes, and you have a lovely cake—oops, I mean, story.

When we boil story down to its essentials, all stories are the same. It's the details that get shuffled around.

Such tightly-controlled stories that follow obvious patterns can be very comforting to readers who need to escape the stress of work or hectic family lives. I've read a lot of these, whether in the form of category romances or cozy mysteries or Shakespearean tragedies or modern meaninglessness (the latter two as have-to's during my career). It's actually easier to read modern meaninglessness than an Agatha Christie. She hides her clues better than they do. (Yes, I'm being snarky.)

~ Plots are Designs ~

Every design has a foundation. Look upon the plot as the foundation of your story. Are you going all glass modern or turreted Victorian? Gingerbread cottage or Federal style? Big city brownstone or white-painted farmhouse? Urban loft or Southwest Adobe?

No matter which style, the building has a foundation, subfloor, walls, ceilings, stairways, windows, doors, cabinetry, flooring—carpet and wood, vinyl and tile, brick and slate. Design the main events of your story based on a worthy plot structure, and the details fall into place.

And it's the details where creativity lies.

Being a Pantster on Plot

A pantster is a writer who launches into story without any planning.

The first method described is how pantsters operate. A situation sparks, a character intrigues, so they launch into the story with no idea where it's going.

Dean Wesley Smith, an advocate of pantstering, calls this method *Writing into the Dark*. https://www.deanwesleysmith.com/writing-into-the-dark-a-new-online-workshop/

Writing without knowing where the story is going opens up the creative, intuitive side of the brain. It prevents the lock-step story that leads to so many books being just alike, without changes.

Pantsters balance serendipitous inspiration with writing themselves into corners, with protagonists who refuse to behave, and minor characters who take over stories.

This is good. This is bad. And this can be very bad.

The good side of pantstering? It unlocks creativity.

We spend much of our lives letting our analytical side control us. Our dreams—especially the weird ones with upside-down yellow airplanes, half-reality and half-impossibility—may be the only time we let the symbolic side talk of us.

The bad side of pantstering? It locks up our writing.

Once we start waiting on the creative spark or kindled inspiration or the "muse of fire" (Shakespeare's *Henry V*), we start locking up words and rarely get anything actually written. We wind up with lots of ideas that have lost their fires and never become finished stories.

Here's the # 1 error of people waiting on inspiration: each sentence has to be perfect.

No, it doesn't have to be perfect. This should be the # 1 certainty for today and all time: Writers rewrite.

The horrific side of pantstering? No, it's not corners and behavior problems and juggernauts. Each one of those teach us about our stories.

Corners and behavior problems and juggernauts are actually good things. When you write yourself into a corner, go back about 10 or 20 or even 50 pages and discover where things went wrong and why they went wrong and how to work around the corner or blast through it. Or when to trash those pages and continue anew. Follow the same process for misbehaving protagonists and dominating walk-ons.

And don't miss the "why they went wrong". This is powerful. The reason events and characters become uncontrollable is because they need to be doing something other than what you've written.

So, if story problems aren't the horror of pantstering, what is? The out-of-control story. The story that goes nowhere or keeps going or is scattered all over the place.

While my dream is to one day meander around backroads with no destination in mind, my intention is to reach a good or worthy destination. Half-impossibility, half-reality.

~ Why are you writing? ~

To tell a story? Stories have ends, with lessons attached ~ just like Aesop's Fables.

To please yourself? Just keep swimming, just keep swimming, flowing with the current, aiming for anything that catches your eye and distracts you.

Being a Plotter on Plot

Sounds like a drug, doesn't it? Sounds like "plodder", doesn't it? This is the charge that is often leveled by pantsters against plotters (the Bullies. Both of them.): Plot is robotic. Plot is boring. Plot kills my creativity.

Yes. Maybe. No!

Plot—whichever method is used creates a rhythm in the story. Pacing. Timing. Flows.

This is what you want for your story, correct? For readers to remember it long after they've closed your book and gone about the rest of their lives.

Pleasure abounds in the draft when writers know what needs to happen and when. Meet a mentor here, get a reward there, face returned evil over there[25]. Simple it is not. Plotters balance structured events with 1] strong character development, 2] antagonists who never surprise with their evil, and 3] a bit of boredom from knowing what's next.

This is good. This can be bad. And this can be very bad.

The good side of plotting? The writer knows what's next.

Writing downtime rarely occurs. With a good outline, time spent writing is merely turning ideas into sentences and paragraphs and chapters. The project gradually turns into a book.

When it's done, no drastic revision is necessary. Finding the story in an erratic jumble of scenes (which happens when pantstering) isn't necessary; the story has unfolded in a logical manner. A little clean-up is all that's needed.

The bad side of plotting? We writers developed all these details of a backstory and character personality, especially the protagonist and antagonist, and we want to see everything we did land on the page.

That would be fatal. Info-dump can kill a story. As soon as we stop showing and cheat by telling, we lose our readers. We want everyone to see how much work we've done; we forget that our job is to entertain and not to exhibit the labor of the story-telling.

The horrific Side of plotting? Ennui with the story we need to unfold.

Boredom is a story-killer. We know everything. We follow our plot lock-step and never meander down any side trials that aren't in the outline. We may

---

[25] three of the 12 stages of the Archetypal Story Pattern

have a flash of inspiration, but it disrupts so many things that we just let that creative dash go.

The worst horror of all? We grow to hate our perfectly plotting and so well-developed story and never finish it.

Pantster and Plotter

Whichever method you adhere to, stop it NOW.

The great crime of both methods is the same: the unfinished story.

Here's the surprise ~ pantsters need plotting and plotters need pantstering.

Pantsters need to consider structure, and plotters need to park of that creative dash. We have to cross the dividing line. Our stories are enriched when we bring the best of both sides into harmony. The three sevens for dreaming a story into reality (in chapter 1) develop a creative plot.

Oh, the slugfest that is the first draft still remains. No matter what we do, with every manuscript, that devious first draft will try to conquer us. We can't let it. We won't let it.

Plot the book. Develop the characters.

While we're writing, whenever we find a pied piper, we need to follow it. Oh sure, we may need to gut some carefully plotted scenes. Sometimes that pied piper sounds pretty but is a little off-tune. Yet we should follow that piping song; it keeps the writing fresh and keeps us enchanted with our story.

Chapter 4 ~ One Ancient Greek :: Aristotle Rocks Characters

A man who lived over 2,400 years ago understood characters better than many modern writers.

For writers beginning to **Think / Pro** and converting from a hobby writer to a professional writer, the ancient Greek philosopher Aristotle seems like a wrong turn. Especially when we're looking at the characters.

Geez, what could he possibly know? I mean, Aristotle[26] is over two thousand years old. Really old. Decrepit. What on earth can someone so old tell me about story?

I grew up with movies and TV. I have computers. And I drive a car. He had a banging *chariot* and scratched on something called papyrus. He didn't even have good paper and ink. What does he know?

That was my thought process. I've learned better.

I've learned not to re-invent the wheel. I've learned to learn from those who have gone before, which is the theme for this chapter.

---

[26] You're likely wondering "Who is Aristotle?" The teacher in me promises to be brief. Have you heard of Alexander the Great? Aristotle taught him. Plato taught Aristotle. Socrates taught Plato. Socrates lived at the time of the three great Greek dramatists, so Aristotle grew up hearing about these three and debating at Plato's Academy with other students on how these three were great and what made them so great.
Socrates, Plato, and Aristotle, by the way, are called the three greatest philosophers who ever lived. Socrates challenged our thought processes. He famously said, "I only know that I know nothing," basically telling us doubt leads to knowledge. Plato challenged our view of the world. He told us to question what we think is reality and remember that what we think is solid importance is merely shadows. Aristotle? He challenged everything.

And Aristotle? Why is he important? Well, he was one of the very first people to look at writing to learn about writing. And that old geeky Greek was smart.

Aristotle[27] examined successful dramas in order to discover the reason they were successful. Those dramas had certain commonalities which are the reason those ancient dramas still grip our modern hearts. Over and over, these stories resonant with people in many different places and across many different times.

Great stories are composed by great story-tellers, and that's what Aristotle studied. He was the first, and everyone since him has merely worked on the foundation he built.

What do the commonalities have in common? (Yes, that's deliberate.) They revealed character. Heart. Personality. Motivation. Behavior. Real-ness.

Everything that we modern writers try so hard to do as we strive to become great storytellers.

Aristotle on Structure

Okay, let's get to the heart of it.

Aristotle views any story's plot from a dramatic standpoint—which comes through the primary tragic character.

He didn't initiate this dramatic plot structure. Instead, he analyzed the best plays, selecting from the best of the best, which were written two and three generations before his life.

The best dramatists for Aristotle—and still recognized as the best in all drama of classical antiquity--were the three award-winning masters: Sophocles (d. 406 BCE), Euripides (d. 406 BCE), and Aeschylus (d. 456 BCE). Their intuitive understanding of the five essentials for great story can affect us just as strongly over 2,000 years later.

While their plays were taken from ancient myth, they weren't telling the stories. They were focused on the people in crisis. People in crisis reveal their true selves. The essences of their personalities—with all the ugly motivations

---

[27] For more information about how Aristotle and other ancient Greeks (and Romans) still influence writing, check out *Old Geeky Greeks: Write Stories with Ancient Techniques*, by M.A. Lee with assistance from Emily R. Dunn, available at online distributors.

and cravings—drive people like Medea & Jason and Antigone & Oedipus and Clytemnestra & Agamemnon.

Flowing from the Greek dramatists' pens are horrible deeds driven by dark revenge, the worst of who we are confronting the noblest that we can be.

People in crisis create powerful suspense. Their motivations form strong speeches as they work out what has happened and what they must do. While the plays *Medea* and *Antigone* are memorable, they contain elements that gripped my heart every single time I taught them.

Agony and ugly motivations are like evil imaginings—until we see similar actions in modern society. To punish her husband who abandoned her, Medea kills her own children (along with a couple of other people). Today, we read headlines about mothers who murder their children, like Susan Smith.

Even as the tragedies present writhing evil, elements of the stories and in the comedies give us light and hope. Antigone has a noble cause and righteous anger on her side, and the audience roots for her even as we know she takes an irrevocable step that will doom her.

The power of these stories easily translates to characters who confront tragic events and rise above them, to triumph rather than die. Some characters reach their destiny, not their doom.

And Aristotle, centuries ago, discovered for us the basic essentials that are revelatory for characters.

Although he didn't present his thesis in quite this manner, we can boil his insights into 5 Essentials and 5 types of characters.

5 Essentials in Structure to Reveal Character

While we can view the 5 Essentials of Structure as plot elements, they are actually requirements for character development. These five open up the characters for the audience. To illustrate each essential, I'll use Shakespeare's *Romeo and Juliet*, a story that many adults worldwide are familiar with.

And stay with me. Don't let weird words weird you out.

Mimesis

The story must imitate life. Stories improve when people behave as they reasonably would, even in fantastical scenarios and settings.

Mythical tropes should follow that trope or explain clearly the reason for any change. Vampires who sparkle in daylight would be more logical if the reason they can enter sunlight (even the dulled sun of the Pacific Northwest in rainy season) is their "vegetarianism".

To most adults looking back at the story, *Romeo and Juliet* couldn't possibly happen, yet the daily news provides us constant examples. Modern updates to the tragedy of the Montagues and the Capulets place the story in a conflict of ethnicity (*West Side Story*) or religion (the Israeli / Palestinian conflict) or economic disparity (*Atonement*).

Shakespeare builds his families as similar, "both alike in dignity" (Prologue to Act I) and provides additional clues that they are focused on monetary gain ("Whoever marries her will have the chinks", I). The original event may have been a business deal gone wrong.

Whatever the inciting event, conflict between the two families can occur and still does. People gossip about such fights all the time.

Are the primary characters imitations of life?

Juliet is the young obedient daughter who finally encounters someone she wants more than she wants to be obedient. She and Romeo speak the same language. Look at their conversation as they dance: both speak of prayer and pilgrims and holy kisses.

In the balcony scene, Juliet admits this love is "too rash, too unadvised, too sudden. / Too like the lightning which doth cease to be / Ere one can say 'it lightens'." (II). She's applying logic to love, yet love isn't logical.

Romeo is a little older than Juliet, yet not much more. He's enough in the world that he recognizes how rare their connection is. Beauty alone does not attract him; their conversation while dancing proves their compatibility. He understands he's courting danger, yet like Juliet he has encountered someone worth the risk.

Both young lovers have extreme reactions to a banishment intended as mercy. Both contemplate suicide. This is typical of fallacious teen-aged thinking.

1. No one has ever felt this way before. They are unique.
2. Doing something secretly adds to the excitement.
3. Waiting and patience are for fuddy-duddies.

4. The world ends when they can't get what they want. Separation is death.
5. Conflict with parents (and others) is to be avoided at all cost. Secrets are better.
6. Barriers require extreme measures to overcome.

While a seasoned person will find a way around any barricade and accept conflict as necessary to achieve a great goal, teenagers cry doom and die.

Yes, indeed, Shakespeare has appropriately imitated teen-aged life.

Peripeteia

In ancient Greek, this word means "falling around", and it represents the unexpected reversal or the sudden change in circumstance :: irony.

Life is filled with ironies. A story will not have *mimesis* if it limits ironic circumstances.

Briefly and succinctly, irony is *the difference between what is expected and what actually occurs*. The three primary types are ~

1. Verbal: saying one thing while meaning another, with the Southernism "Bless her heart" as an example when the exact opposite is meant. "Don't you look pretty", when an ink mark crosses the face, is an obvious example. Sarcasm is not an exact synonym of Verbal Irony; the heavy mockery of sarcasm is intended to ridicule.
2. Situational: actions that cause an unintended or unexpected effect. This is not coincidence. Just married and anticipating only good things, Romeo in ten short minutes causes the death of his best friend Mercutio and deliberately murders Tybalt. These events are the unintended and unexpected conclusion to Tybalt's challenge of Romeo (III). Juliet tries to return to her father's good will by saying she will obey him only to have him move up her marriage to Count Paris (IV).
3. Dramatic: In this irony, the audience knows information that the characters do not. The audience sees Juliet's mother approaching as the two newlyweds say goodbye (III). We know that Juliet is not really dead while Romeo does not. We know that she is on the verge of waking up— her colors is returning. Romeo even says, "Thy lips are warm"—and we want to cry "wait" as he commits suicide (V).

Hamartia (and Hubris)

Hamartia is the fatal flaw leading to the protagonist's downfall.

Most modern character development templates mention a character's weakness.

Indiana Jones' fear of snakes is legendary. *Raiders of the Lost Ark* uses this fear effectively. We are introduced to it early, with the snake in the seat of the airplane as it takes off from the river in the South American jungle. That fear becomes suspenseful when Indy encounters the hundreds of snakes in the Egyptian tomb.

Fear, however, is insufficient as a fatal flaw. A fatal flaw for a character should be a mistaken way of thinking.

Harry Potter in J.K. Rowling's' series invariably thinks that he can handle a problem by himself. Time and time again he discovers that he needs Hermione and Ron.

Romeo's fatal flaw is his violent emotions.

- His love is too extreme: he cannot contemplate life without Juliet.
- His plans are too extreme: rather than enlisting Prince Escalus as the mediator of a marriage that can end the feud, Romeo plots a secret marriage.
- His anger is too extreme: he murders Tybalt when just 15 minutes prior he was refusing to accept a challenge to a duel.

Juliet's fatal flaw is her dependence on others.

- She is the obedient daughter, wholly dependent on her parents. She falls in with their plans for her future until she meets Romeo.
- She is then dependent on Romeo's plan for their marriage.
- Finally, she is dependent on Friar Lawrence's plan to avoid her coming marriage to Count Paris.

A special kind of *hamartia* is *hubris*. In ancient Greece, this was the pride that challenges fate or the gods or circumstance. Not all *hamartia* is *hubris*, but all *hubris* is *hamartia*.

Hubris occurs when someone believes that they can do no wrong. They are equal to the gods.

Part of the reason Aristotle insists on hubris is his belief that a tragic hero must fall from a great height.

The other part of hubris relates to the vulture-like drive in all humans, to relish and feed on other's great misery. [Watch how drivers and passengers peer so closely when they pass a car wreck. Students encircle two arguing peers in the school corridor.]

With most genre stories, the protagonist will have weaknesses and even tainting secrets yet lack the doom-creating hubris. However, the antagonist or other characters can certainly have weaknesses, secrets, and hubris.

Romeo says, right before his marriage to Juliet, "Love-devouring death do what he dare; it is enough I may but call her mine." Of course, an hour later, after Mercutio and Tybalt are dead, he realizes, "I am fortune's fool!" (III i). He dared Death; Death took the dare and came out the winner.

The protagonist may have arrogance (*hubris*) in thinking an extreme danger (to a relationship, to a community, to personal advancement) will not happen to them. Or s/he will be blind to circumstances (*hamartia*) that create the extreme danger.

Catastrophe

That great height from which a character falls increases the catastrophe. This disaster must be one from which no recovery seems possible.

In modern fiction, with its triumph over the conflict, an ordeal is necessary. The only difference between Oedipus or Macbeth with a modern protagonist is. . .well, there is no real difference when you think about it.

Romeo's banishment does not seem like a horrible event. After all, Prince Escalus showed mercy; he could have executed Romeo as he had decreed he would execute the next fighters. However, both Romeo and Juliet consider banishment as equal to death, and they threaten suicide.

Juliet's (supposed) death becomes a suicidal catastrophe for Romeo. As soon as he hears about it, he schemes a method to kill himself. His suicide upon Juliet's moment of awakening becomes her catastrophe.

Romeo and Juliet is often classified as a pathetic tragedy since the action of neither protagonist bring about their doom. They are driven to their deaths more by the ticking of a clock than by their own actions. Yet Shakespeare has created two juveniles who consider no other recourse for their love except an extreme one. He has carefully created the "violent delights" which lead to their "violent ends".

Then Shakespeare takes his catastrophe one step further. Romeo's banishment and subsequent suicide lead to the death of his mother; only his father remains alive, and the name and house will die with him. Juliet's family is in a similar case, for the cousin Tybalt is now dead and her father is played as an old man, broken by the end of the play, with little more to drive him forward. Prince Escalus' relative, Count Paris, is also dead.

The feud between the two families has caused widespread disaster. Only Benvolio is absent at the end of the play.

And where is Benvolio at the end of the play? Did he travel to Mantua with Romeo and was left behind when Romeo returned to Verona? Did he succumb to infection from the wound he received in the opening street fight between the Montagues and the Capulets? The audience is given no clues. Benvolio is gone—just as the two families are now gone.

Catharsis

Simply defined, catharsis is *purging, cleansing*. In story, it requires more than an emotional, heart-wrenching end. It must contain an intellectual acceptance by the audience, or the story has not achieved its purpose.

The Latin poet Horace, centuries after Aristotle, redefined the closing purpose of catharsis as "dulce et utile", sweetness and usefulness. The story should be sweet entertainment even as it presents useful enlightenment. We the audience and readers need to know that the suffering we endured with the characters had purpose.

Suffering's purpose creates investment by the audience into our characters. Using *dulce et utile* deepens the story. With *peripeteia,* writers examine how the world turns against their main character. *Hubris* seeds a doom of the protagonist's own making, even though s/he may not see that doom approaching.

Throughout *Romeo and Juliet,* Friar Lawrence warns that "violent delights lead to violent ends." Shakespeare is not telling a love story; he is explaining how good reason can be overcome by emotions. Even the voice of reason, the Friar, is overcome by fear in the last act. He could have intervened if he had been on time. We may be unhappy with the ending of the play, but we should be accepting of it. And thus, we the audience have three lessons, lessons we are still trying to learn today:

- Use reason first.
- Moderate all emotions.
- Intervene on time; don't hesitate.

We see many more lessons as well. And once we understand these lessons, we can accept the deaths in Shakespeare's tragedy: Romeo, Juliet, Mercutio,

Tybalt, Lady Montague, and Count Paris. Six dead. And maybe Benvolio, who makes seven.

Catharsis is achieved.

The Essentials Have Purpose

While Aristotle focused on tragedy, most modern fiction aims for a successful culmination of the conflict. Literary fiction is distinguished from genre fiction by that single word *successful*. Yet even in non-tragic literary fiction, life as it was may be destroyed in order to allow a new birth of hope for the future. Without catastrophe and catharsis, the protagonist of hopeful literary fiction will not achieve their climb from disaster.

Genre writers will discover that these five essentials still fit their mysteries or action-adventures or romances. A character fulfilling his destiny will face these five and overcome them, achieving the desired goal and being transformed in the journey.

Keep Aristotle's 5 Essentials at the forefront as you develop your primary characters and place them in your selected plot method.

Aristotle on Characters

Earlier, we took a quick glance at characters. Once you have your story started and you know it's going to be a story, you need to stop and deepen your characters, so they will live and breathe. Characters drive plot. When first we writers consider a situation, the character who confronts it is what we find intriguing.

Beyond the protagonist, Aristotle gives us four more essential character types to support and to oppose the primary character.

The Greek word *agon* is translated as *conflict*. When the primary character is called the *protagonist*, we see that *agon* at the center of the word. This reminds us that conflict should be at the center of your primary character's development and story arc.

Agon gives us the modern word "agony". Any characters involved in the conflict should agonize over their actions and reactions to events and other characters. Our protagonists, especially, should agonize when they must sacrifice something dear in order to achieve their desired goals.

Today, when we refer to characters in opposition to the protagonist, we refer to them as *antagonists*. The Greek *agon* is also at the center of this word. The antagonist was not a specialized term in Aristotle's day. Instead of *antagonist* we'll examine two character terms that you may find new (and then I give a little bit more about modern antagonists).

Protagonist

The protagonist is the primary character facing the conflict. *Pro-*is a prefix for "confronting". With the *agon*, the protagonist is clearly the primary character *confronting the conflict*. This reminds us to keep our protagonist active, not drifting or reeling from situation to situation.

While the weaknesses and the fatal flaws of *hamartia* are good, better for our protagonists would be deep-seated fears that drive them away from the action they must take.

When I say 'fear', I am not talking about agoraphobia or claustrophobia or even mysophobia (fear of germs). These are strong irrational fears that cause panic attacks.

I am talking about **secrets**. Give to your primary characters a secret or two that they are highly motivated to keep. The revelation of the secret would destroy them not only publicly but personally, both their outward lives and their inward images of themselves.

The secrets should connect to haunting past events, often called **ghosts**. That past taints their present as well as everything they plan for the future. And the characters will twist themselves into pretzels to stop any revelation.

The secrets' stain should plant a seed of corruption in every aspect of their life.

Antagonist

Any antagonist—the primary conflict-creator—should seek a goal that is mirrored to the protagonist. Their conflict may occur over the same treasure, the same career advancement, or the same approbation from the community. The antagonist may want the destruction of what the protagonist is trying to create. S/he will twist any concept that the protagonist developed to improve the world.

Both protagonist and antagonist should work equally hard to achieve their goals. They are in a constant push-pull synergy.

In looking at Aristotle's lessons, we are reminded that the best creators of *agon* are good people trying to do good things. For Aristotle, the antagonist did not exist as a character (conflict came from within). Instead, he presents these following two characters as necessary for dramatic situations:

Deuteragonist

Deuter = second. Agon = conflict.

The deuteragonist originally came on the ancient Greek stage to confront the protagonist with a second dilemma in addition to facing her/his own conflict.

This character is not a villain. S/he is just like us, trying to make good decisions, trying to do what's best.

However, the road to Hell is paved with good intentions. Good intentions are not enough. They can and do lead to us offering people a "free pass" only to have them commit greater evils. Good intentions often keep us from acting when we should, primarily because we are trying to be "nice".

The perfect example is Corinth's king Creon, in the ancient drama of *Medea*. His daughter has recently married Jason, Medea's love and husband (although Jason claimed that a barbaric marriage didn't count). Creon wants to protect his daughter from Medea's wrath. He wants to protect his city. Medea's past murders are well known. To help Jason, she killed her own brother and his uncle.

Creon knows that he must get rid of Medea. The easiest choice is to have her executed, but she hasn't actually committed a crime in his city (just elsewhere). He decides she must leave, and so he orders Medea and her children into exile.

Now, Creon himself was an exile. He knows how difficult being outcast and alone are. He knows what happens to those who are weak and without protection. He knows that Medea and her children will starve. They will be helpless prey for men and beasts. Therefore, with the best of intentions, Creon gives Medea a half-day before she must leave.

He thinks she will use it to hire protection and gather supplies and liquidate any assets that she cannot take with her.

He doesn't know she will use it to set in motion a horrific plan that will lead to his daughter's terrible death, his own death when he tries to save his daughter, and the deaths of the children of Jason and Medea. (Yes, Medea killed her own children. She's evil.)

Another example of a *deuteragonist* is Friar Lawrence in *Romeo and Juliet*. He wants to help the two young lovers. He believes that marrying them will end the feud. These are worthy intentions. Thus, he agrees to perform the marriage ceremony, even though it occurs in secret and he really has no authority to perform it. (He's a friar, not a priest.)

In trying to do good he participates in a lie and a crime, the secret marriage and the impersonation of a priest.

The friar also gives Juliet the potion that will put her in a death-like sleep. He does this, so she can avoid a bigamous marriage. This is an even worthier intention.

However, the letter he sent to Romeo in Mantua, which would have explained that Juliet was not dead, never reaches its destination. Romeo hears of Juliet's death, and thus begins the chain of events that will lead to three more deaths.

Tritagonist

Tri = third. Agon = conflict. Just like the deuteragonist, the *tritagonist* presents a third conflict for the protagonist even as this character confronts a conflict of his own.

Here we have another good person, trying to do the right thing only to suffer because of their good intentions.

Also from the ancient Greek drama *Medea*, we have the character of Aegeus, who has no son and therefore no heir to the throne of Athens. He is a former friend of Jason and knows Medea because of him. Newly arrived and caught up in his own troubles, he doesn't really know what's been happening between Jason and Medea and at the palace.

When Medea tells him that she must enter exile, Aegeus basically says, "That's bad." When she says that people who hurt others should be punished, he basically says, "That's what you would think." And when she says, "Let's make a bargain. You give me protection in Athens, and I'll ensure you have a son," he agrees. Then she makes him swear that, if he goes back on his vow of protection, he will only see blackness in the sky. Now Aegeus is worried, but he swears.

His agony comes many years later, in the story of Theseus. When his yet-unknown son arrives in Athens, he wants Medea to poison the young hero.

She agrees. Fortunately, he recognizes his son in time. And Medea is banished from Athens.

Theseus then goes to Crete, to prevent King Minos from sacrificing Athenian youth to the minotaur. He successfully defeats the monster and returns home.

Aegeus awaits the return of his only son and heir on the cliff. From that great height he will see the ship's return. If Theseus succeeded, he was to raise white sails on the ship. If Theseus dies, black sails will fly.

Theseus forgets to change the sails. When he sees only blackness in the sky, Aegeus leaps to his death, thinking his only son and heir is dead.

In *Romeo and Juliet*, three characters serve as examples of the *tritagonist*. These three are Mercutio, Benvolio, and Count Paris. (They are also foils for Romeo, mirroring a certain element of his character.)

Let's focus on Count Paris. He loved Juliet and wanted to marry her. However, Juliet's marriage to Paris would be bigamous: she is already married to Romeo. Thus, Paris creates a dilemma for her. She does not want to break man's law about marriage; nor does she want to break the law of her, which is devoted to Romeo. She runs to Friar Lawrence for help, and he gives her the death-like sleep potion.

The proof we have of Count Paris' love of Juliet comes at the end. Believing she is dead, he is placing flowers at her tomb, a nightly vigil. When he sees Romeo coming, he recognizes that here is the man who caused her such grief that she died.

He confronts Romeo who warns Paris that he has nothing to lose. He draws a sword and demands Romeo leave the site of the tomb. Obviously, he thinks Romeo has come to desecrate the body of his enemy Tybalt.

Romeo, of course, no longer cares what he does in this life. His only intention is to die beside Juliet, their bodies lying together in the tomb. Their confrontation quickly becomes another sword fight (the third in the play). Paris is no match for Romeo. Wounded fatally, he cries, "Lay me beside Juliet." Poor guy.

Antagonist 5 + 5 + 5

We usually view the antagonist as one of several types of villains; however, we need to remember the roles of the deuteragonist and the tritagonist. Not all people are evil. Not all people want to hurt others. Most people in a community want to help their fellows.

Nevertheless, a presentation of antagonists would not be complete without a brief acknowledgement of modern conflict-creators.

5 Forms of Conflict

- Man vs. Man ~ *Godfather II*
- Man vs. Self ~ *Wild*
- Man vs. Nature (which has further developed into Technology/Machine) ~ *Castaway*
- Man vs. Society ~ *The Hunger Games*
- Man vs. God (which extends into the supernatural realm as well as any discussion of ancient evil) ~ *Interview with the Vampire*

5 Simple Antagonists

We see these most often because they are easy to set up and knock down.

- Villain ~ over-the-top bad guy. the classic example is Snidely Whiplash in *the Dudley Do-right cartoons*.
- Straw Man ~ a character set up as a one-sided evil who is easy to defeat. *The Devil wears Prada*
- Bully ~ the stereotypical bully tries to intimidate those who are weaker. When confronted, the bully runs away like a coward. *The Karate Kid*
- Beast ~ large and dangerous, feared because the primary motivation is animal-based and thus lacks human mercy (food, predator hunting prey). *Jaws* or *The Grey*
- Alien ~ the off-world stranger, with unknown strengths and motivations, unknown weaknesses and reactions. *Alien* or *Predator.*

5 Not-Simple Antagonists

Most writers do not write these not-simple evil-doers as they truly are. They back off once the story gets going. When writers do follow through, we readers and audience get a memorable story that others try and try to imitate.

- The Corrupted ~ *Anatomy of a Murder* or *Whatever Happened to Baby Jane?*
- The Femme Fatale ~ *Basic Instinct*
- The Mastermind ~ *Terminator*
- The Criminal ~ Moriarty in the new *Sherlock* series
- The Disturbed ~ *Hannibal*

Of course, the best antagonist is not an antagonist at all ~ **the Perfect Person** ~ Mary Crawford in the 2007 *Mansfield Park*.

Chorus

In ancient Greece, the Chorus truly was a group "singing" or chanting to the audience. The chorus even began with choreographed steps.

Primarily, though, the Chorus interacted with the protagonist, providing reactions to the protagonist and information for the audience.

In modern stories, the Chorus has become side characters who 1] illuminate information or 2] bolster and support the protagonist or 3] serve as a minion of the antagonist. These side characters reveal the primary characters through their interactions.

Classically, the Chorus has three roles:

1. provide exposition: background, situation. For example, a *mentor* who makes the protagonist examine what's been and what could be.
2. provide social commentary and expected reactions, emotional and logical, such as the good friend, the *confidante*.
3. announce entrances. The character who says, "Who is that person?" Info-dump can ruin a story. Writers can instead use dialogue to present the information through conversation. This avoids the author rattling words onto the page and boring the reader. (Of course, the best way to "info-dump" is to scatter it through the story.)

Here's my list of characters designed to illuminate your protagonist and antagonist. Add them to the list of 5 + 5 + 5 villains for conflict, and you have 25 lovely side characters to pick and choose from.

10 Types of Side Characters

- Threshold Guardian ~ determined to block the protagonist's passage
- Ally ~ the helpful and worthy friend who always has the protagonist's back
- Foil ~ a character who in many respects is just like the protagonist. (You can have more than one. In *Romeo and Juliet*, Shakespeare had four for Romeo: Mercutio, Benvolio, Paris, and Tybalt.) Foils will highlight the protagonist's weakness or flaw and fail to stand against the trial that undermines that weakness. Thus, their failure helps the protagonists prepare for their own test. (Boromir and Aragorn in *The Fellowship of the Ring*)
- Love Interest ~ In old stories, the woman that the protagonist loved was often merely a walk-on character. Now the love interest is a woman side-by-side with the man. Even better, the woman is the protagonist, and the

man is the love interest.

- Blocking Figure ~ characters who have the best intentions for the protagonist but stand in the way. Juliet's parents are great examples.
- Idol ~ the character that the protagonist has looked up to but who is revealed as having clay feet.
- Jokester ~ He plays to an audience. He doesn't care about the audience's derision, as long as he is getting laughter. His actions are actually reactions, a cyclical feeding off the audience.
- Trickster ~ a character who thinks himself clever, but his actions only cause problems for everyone else. Ulysses is a trickster: He successfully finds a way to get his men out of the cave of the cyclops before another one can be eaten. He also managed to blind the monster to ensure their escape. Enraged at being blinded and losing his dinner, the cyclops chucks boulders around, hoping to injure the men who escaped him. And this is where Ulysses reveals his arrogance about being clever. He must tell the cyclops who blinded him. In doing so, he gives the cyclops a direction to aim the boulders—and nearly sinks the ship they are escaping on. And then the cyclops prays to his ancestor Poseidon to punish Ulysses; Poseidon does so. (Ulysses is a clever idiot. That's a simple explanation for trickster.)
- Shapeshifter ~ comes in two forms. Form One: the character that is trusted who is actually working for the antagonist. Form Two: the character that no one trusts who is actually very trustworthy. In a previous chapter, I referred to this characters as the seeming ally (SAlly).

Deus ex Machina

Aristotle's last character to include in every story is the Deus ex Machina (DexM). Literally, this is the "god out of the machine".

In ancient Greek dramas, sometimes the protagonist would have no possible way out of the dilemma. Enter the DexM. A god would intervene, providing some miracle that kept the hero from dying.

Audiences in Aristotle's time loved the DexM. The ancient Greeks celebrated the god's arrival as a religious experience. The dramas, of course, were part of a religious ceremony, running for several days. This means that the DexM would be celebrated for saving the day, like a Mighty Mouse come to rescue when no other rescue was humanly possible.

Modern audiences and readers, however, frown upon such sudden, unanticipated escapes. They consider it a weakness by the writer.

We call DexM a coincidence. When coincidence is unexplained or unexpected, the logical part of our *catharsis* is unexplained and unacceptable.

The best example of the infuriating DexM is a mystery when the detective suddenly finds out the answer through a letter (or other clue) not shared with the reader. "All is now clear," the detective declares. Well, to her it is. As for the rest of us, we change the channel or throw the book across the room (print version, not the ebook).

An example of the outside hand saving a character recently occurred in the excellent TV series *Vera*. This police procedural is based on the books by Ann Cleeves. A DexM occurs in series 2, episode 4.

The dead drug dealer's son stops the dead drug addict's mother from committing suicide. As she lost her purpose when she lost her son, he lost his purpose in trying to connect to his now-murdered father. DexM occurs by placing him on the bridge just as she climbs the railing to jump off the bridge.

It's a neat juxtaposition: He needs parenting; she needs a child. He saved her physical life; she will save his intellectual and emotional life. But the DexM nags at us. It's a weakness that could be resolved with foreshadowing. Cleeves likely resolved the issue in her book; the foreshadowing may have been cut from the teleplay.

When we resort to coincidence or an outside hand that saves the protagonist or any character from doom (or causes the doom when it could be avoided), then we should set it up with foreshadowing.

Foreshadowing

In an ancient story, the hero would call upon the god to save him. He would make an offering, and an eerie response to that offering (such as the fire leaping three times) would show a god actively aware of the hero. Another such touch in the center of the story—such as a fog mysteriously blowing away—would set up the god's continued involvement. Nothing more need be done.

In a modern story, the protagonist could escape doom by the timely arrival of a subway or the inconvenient friend's visit or the scary neighbor who's not as evil as the antagonist. Of course, the scary neighbor—lifting weights in the hall, cleaning his gun on the balcony shared with the protagonist, bandaging a wounded arm—could just as easily work for the antagonist.[28]

The subway's arrival can be foreshadowed by having the protagonist take it

---

[28] Now I want to write this, but as a rescue, not a deepened doom.

into the town much earlier in the story. The inconvenient friend can drop in early and in the story's middle, just as the protagonist needs to be somewhere else. Then both subway and inconvenient friend can re-appear at the necessary moment.

As a writer, when you discover a DexM is needed, in this lovely age of computers it is easy to add foreshadowing. The key is to keep the foreshadowed elements as simple shadows, brief touches, noticed and gone—in the same way mystery writers plant clues and red herrings.

Wrapping Up

With these early essentials, Aristotle provides us with tons of assistance in understanding well-written characters. This Geeky Greek may be ancient, but he rocked the foundations of character for us. And for that, Aristotle still rocks.

Chapter 5 ~ One Simple Injunction: Writer's Block Doesn't Exist

*Look at that chapter title again—Writer's Block does **NOT** exist.*

I'm speaking heresy in the writing community.

Do you know someone who claims to suffer from Writer's Block? Have you yourself ever said, "I am blocked. I can't write anything."

I have struggled many, many times with that ailment. I even believed that diagnosis for a few years. Because no words would come for my fiction, I thought I was blocked . . . even as I wrote lesson plans and created quizzes and composed emails.

And then a couple of things dawned on me.

The first dawning came in my search to end my own block. I realized that "block" meant *to be unable to put words on the page.*

That certainly wasn't the problem. I could put words on the page. That's when I discovered that true Writer's Block is an impossibility.

The second dawning came when I saw that major life crossroad coming. (You know, the major crossroad that I described in the Introduction.)

I thought of all the ways that I had pursued excellence in my job performance (a job that I enjoyed even though parts of it were hell.) If ever I were to achieve my dream of writing professionally, I would need to pursue excellence in my job performance of writing.

Writing needed to become my focus.

With the approach of that major crossroad, I needed to choose. Did I want to continue devoting all my brain energies and creativity to a job that would soon end? Or did I want to pursue my dream?

Time for the dream.

Oh, I still devoted myself to my job during the work hours, yet I began to scrupulously maintain the compartments of work and home. I refused to take work home with me. I set up a plan, I set up long-term and short-term goals, and I began to change the focus of my off hours. Brain-tired, energy-zapped, creativity-sucked, I still managed to put words on the page when I came home from work and finished the day's obligations. 250 words. Then 500 words. 1,000 words after work became a celebration. Many Saturdays became blissful days because I woke fresh and could spend the day writing in two-hour increments: 8-10, 1-3, 4-6, 8-10.

Even on the days when the muse danced away in a dark forest I couldn't reach, I managed words on page. Even when I gutted everything I had written for five straight days, I still achieved. The daily word count worked steadily to build a scene. The scene built into a chapter. Chapters built into a novel.

I met the short-term goals then the long-term goals and kept going.

The Heretical Belief

Heresy is an opinion contrary to generally accepted beliefs (according to Merriam Webster, my go-to dictionary). I'm heretical because I believe it is impossible to suffer from Writer's Block. Truly impossible.

I can hear the clamor for beheading, even as I type away in my little Wren's Nest.

Listen to me now, or you will forever be a victim. Writer's Block is impossible.

Remember the definition of Writer's Block: *to be unable to put words on the page*. Is that impossible for you?

Even when I could not think of a single character in a scene, I could put words on the page. The words might not have been ones that I wanted to write, but I was still composing lesson plans, creating—out of my head—worksheets on figurative language, guided poetry analysis, and tests.

I composed emails. I wrote letters. I sent messages. I put my name on Christmas cards (I'm old-fashioned).

I was writing, just not the writing that I wanted to do. And the writing that I was doing was sucking all my creative energies.

I started cutting the deep composing that I had always done during my work to save creative energies for my goal. I didn't cut it all, but I cut enough.

Artists can paint. They may not be painting what they want to. They may hate what's on the canvas. It's boring and useless, they may think, drivel rather than art, gimmick rather than truth. But they can apply color to the canvas. That's painting.

You may think you're blocked, but you can compose a FB message or a tweet or an email. You can write a blog, even if in your mind it's boring and useless, drivel rather than art, gimmick rather than truth.

The Truth about Writer's Block

Truth survives gimmickry.

Artists can re-paint. They can change perspective or techniques or even style. They can paint for fun or for anger, to share laughs or to anticipate burning, a ritual bonfire of the drivel. Every stroke of the brush moves them out of the stoppage they found themselves in.

The writer's truth? We also survive gimmickry. We can re-write. Those boring, useless, driveling words? We can apply a new viewpoint or setting or changed outcome of a scene. We can toss off a quick note or pen a diatribe, share it for laughs or get the fire out of our blood, a burning of what angers us and never needs to enter the sunshine. Every keystroke on the laptop moves us out of the stoppage we find ourselves in.

Stoppage does happen. Barriers, blockades, those come up. But don't call them Writer's Block. Don't fall into that fallback mentality.

As writers, we have to be halfway decent at self-analysis. In looking at our foibles and weaknesses and those of other people, we find guides to illuminate our characters' flaws and sins.

Self-analysis can also guide us out of that horrid time that people half-jokingly call Writer's Block.

Don't joke about it; it's truly horrid. But find a way to defeat it.

If we must block anything, we should block the petty upsets of life. We learn to admit when we're wrong and keep moving ahead. When we find ourselves dug into deep holes, we have to figure out ways to climb out.

Whether we're living or writing.

And we constantly look for ways to improve. We may attend conferences and seminars, but we can teach ourselves 10 months of the year. We spend one month on vacation. The other month is for those widely spaced days when we kick and scream at the world we've created.

So, our self-analysis, that's to determine what is this barrier between us and our writing.

When we find ourselves unable to work, we need to diagnose the problem. It's not Writer's Block. Refuse to say that. We can write. We can put words onto the page.

Do You Need Proof?

Try these cure-alls.

~ Go write an email just saying "Hello. I was thinking about you. I think we need to get together for coffee."

Don't back out. Go for coffee.

~ Write an angry poem and burn it afterward. Grant yourself permission to make mistakes and write drivel. And burn it.

Don't back out. Spindle it up and put a match to it.

~ Sit in front of a keyboard, toss out a bunch of words, and hit delete.

Don't back out. Delete.

The key to all three of these: They serve as proof that you can still put words on the page. Proof that you do not have Writer's Block.

Your Muse will be appalled. Ignore her weeping.

Your Imp of Mischief will shout with glee. Laugh with him.

Celebrate words that don't have a purpose.

And offend that pesky muse. Tell her who is in charge. You are. Writers don't wait on inspiration. We have jobs to do.

We're learning to *Think like a Pro*. We're after a *New Advent* for our writing.

Pros have **deadlines.** They have to put out product, no matter what, or they don't get paid. While they know their necessary daily output, they also schedule in a cushion that covers any disruptions.

They learn to **write every day**--always remembering that re-writing is available if it's boring or useless or drivel.

Pros use **models and patterns** that others have developed. They have a process that works for them, but they are perfectly willing to shake up that process if they realize changes are necessary.

Essentials (whether it's the structure that controls a revelatory series of events (plot) or the essentials of specific sets of characters) helps writers understand the size of the project, the major units of the project, and the smaller elements inside each major unit. Pros consider the major structure and the smaller elements that turn individual words into completed projects. When the old patterns aren't working, they seek out new ways to build their story's foundations.

Words aren't the problem. It's the project we're working on. And our attitude toward that project.

We have to diagnose the problem to determine the solution.

I think this barrier or wall between us and our writing can actually fall into three distinct writer's maladies.

Diagnostic Quiz

❧ Select one of the following problems.

   A. You constantly escape from your current project, chasing distractions that prevent your bum from sitting in a chair.
   B. You delay the hard parts of your writing in order to pursue other writing projects.
   C. You keep yawning when you should be writing.

❧ Select the best description of your writing problem.

   A. You find yourself with writing time, but you deliberately place yourself far from your writing space.
   B. You never want to show your writing to anyone because it's not finished.
   C. When you schedule your writing time, you just stare at the screen, with no words in your head.

❧ Select the best mindset that replicates your inner critic.

   A. I have more and more things to do before I can begin writing.
   B. I keep hearing voices from my past, telling me that my writing

will never be good enough.

    C. I don't need to learn anything about writing. These are my words. I won't change them for anyone.

If you selected A for two or all three of the symptoms, then you actually have something called Writer's Refusal.

If you answered with two or three as B, then you have Writer's Procrastination.

If you landed primarily in C, you have the worst condition: Writer's Inertia.

Writer's Refusal

Writer's Refusal is the least of the three mis-identified problems that a writer confronts.

This particular malady occurs when some perverse instinct inside us decides that it doesn't want to do what it knows good and well that it must do.

We chase other things—by video gaming or extending our errands—rather than heading to our writing area and focusing on our primary project. We claim that we have to do laundry then plant ourselves in front of the TV while the washer and dryer work for us. You know, in the 45 minutes that the washer or dryer is running, we can write and polish a scene.

We have set aside time to write. Suddenly, we look around and discover that we're in parts unknown to our writing space. This isn't Writer's Block; this is Refusing to Write.

The writing has lost its first, white-hot allure.

Our refusal to write occurs for two very simple reasons: either we need an escape or an unburdening when we've taken on too much too soon.

Desperate to escape?

Then schedule an escape.

Escape with a Vacay: Take a vacation from writing. Take off for one day—and write about that escape when you climb into bed that night. Anaïs Nin said that we "write to taste life twice, in the moment and in retrospection."[29]

Escape with Play: Write something just for fun. *Something* is always there in our minds. It may not be what we want. It may not be what we can see how to use. Yet it's there. Our subconscious gifted it to us and is demanding that we deal with it. Use it or lose it, the cliché says, and that truth is never truer than with writing.

"Writing just anything that's not about my current project doesn't count," you retort. Wrong. It counts. It's writing, and we're talking about our brains wanting to escape that current project. We can't let our brains escape through a total shut-down. We shouldn't. And we won't.

Escape the Grind: Write something that you know you're going to trash[30]. Whether you delete it or burn it or shred it, just pour words onto the paper, and give yourself the freedom to trash it.

Something needs to come out. If you need to escape the grind of writing, then something is simmering beneath your conscious mind. Simmering and simmering and wanting to boil—and you need to control that simmer.

An Escape Exercise to Try

Pick an evocative word (fear, beginnings, falling leaves, manipulation). Begin writing. Don't stop. Don't edit. Don't re-read. Follow where your brain leads. Don't worry about clichés or song phrases or anything like that. Just write and write and write.

After three to five minutes, you will hit a stop. The brain is throwing up static. To get past the static, write the last word (the one that carries an idea) over and over until a new thought surfaces and follow that one as well. A new thought will surface. Don't judge it; just run with it.

Don't try to be coherent, with all the ideas tied together. Don't try to censor what pours out. Write for 15 solid minutes. Whenever you hit a stop, follow the same procedure as before: repeat then run with the first thought up.

I used to do this exercise with my 9th grade students. To encourage them, I

---

[29] See Note 5.

[30] I would do this **grind-escape** with paper and pen/pencil. The brain has a direct connection to your dominant hand (not to your shared hands on the keyboard, whether you use all fingers or all thumbs). Formation of the letters awakens the brain to activity. Writing words awakens thought. We need to pour out our below-the-surface thoughts, which can only happen if we are pouring straight out of our intuitive side of the brain rather than the critical side.

would write with them. For the first two times, I would read what I had written after we all finished. After that, I would ask for volunteers (and only volunteers) to share what they thought was their best idea. We did this about once a week. If 9th graders who thought they had nothing in their heads can churn out an entire page in 7 minutes, you can do the same.

Here's an example.

My starting word was **Manipulation**. I wrote this, with my students, in April, which means this activity had been running for several months. We were studying William Shakespeare's *Romeo & Juliet*, which is the R & J. I changed Clinton's name. I haven't corrected anything else, just reproduced exactly what I wrote.

> Manipulation. Appropriate manipulation devices. Devices to rid self of unwanted. Poor Clinton. He doesn't use any of our suggestions. mommy manipulation evil stepmother fairy tales like what R & J is based on – with tragic endings. Clinton is too nice. Why is it that women are never attracted to the nice guys nice guys finish last— sugar daddy is a 3rd—nice guys have to work at getting wives. The same as nice girls and then what they get is not what they wanted so they must swallow their anger / discouragement / unhappiness and that affects their health. Love at 1st sight. R had visual lust and proclaimed it love. J fell in love with his wooing. An interesting question, what made these 2 fall in love? How enduring would that love have been? After the initial attraction, how did their love grow and become stronger? Love love love love chemical reaction – hormones gone haywire. Only after do we find commonalities that make us stay attracted. J is entranced by her first kiss R by her beauty. Something makes it more the tug at heart strings, the need for the other, the excitement, adrenaline rush. Infatuation all we have or does it develop into shared experiences that unite two. Love love love lost love lost love lost opportunities. Last opportunities unseized, ungrabbed become lost opportunities. Regrets but last days can also be regret as think of everything will leave, people won't see anymore. Facing life changes. A little scary, anxious, trepidation. A little like birdling taking its last flight from the nest. Practice runs all over.

Now, I write fast, and this exercise had become habit. When I look back in my journal, the writing for early September is half this length. In this passage, you can see where I have twice hit static. I have gone from manipulation to fairy tales and love then lost opportunities and regrets, winding up with a bird leaving its nest and launching into the world. That my brain talking to me, not me talking to my brain.

This exercise gets easier the more you do it. Here's an example from September of that year, much earlier:

The students' word was **Summer's End**. That's not where I started. I was frustrated and looking forward to a weekend trip that would take me away.

> Summer's End. Explaining and explaining what to do. 3 minutes then 3 more minutes, of a simple instruction. Over and over. Like rain pouring down, drop after drop, word after word, idea after idea. Now you're playing? Rain. Weather, how cold will it be? Rain. Need suit, towel, robe, slippers for wet, clothes, minimum makeup, sleeping bad and thermarest, what else? Really lightweight, Nordic bag, want to walk in morning, boots, hiking socks. Slicker? Need to buy a slicker type parka. Now this again was avoidance. 2ce. Play then list. What are you afraid of? What about rain makes you afraid? Rain rain rain rain rain following runlets running down the hillside collecting in ditches run-off gathers little trickles of water that become streams and streams become creeks to rivers to lakes to the sea continuous ocean waves in and out a steady rocking movement cradle breathing tide and spin of earth 2 great forces making the great forces of earth move and drift and shift and affect people daily. Air and water. Breathing. Needing air. Needing others. Need to need to others. Need to learn to rely on others. Need to learn to receive not just give.

I share this to show the difficulty of the exercise but also its revelatory experience. Again, you can see static occur, you can see how I was directing my thoughts with the list before I took myself to task (calling it "avoidance") and forced myself to follow the exercise. Finally, you see how the free-flow of ideas finally led to a significant revelation.

For killing the grind, however, I believe this exercise works best when the free-flow writing lasts for 15 solid minutes. However, the seven-minute exercise can become a weekly habit that will get you in touch with your right-brain creative muse.

Take the escape. After it's over, write about it, journal or blog or free sketch. And the next day, return to your current project.

Never wait on your muse. You are a Pro. You are in charge of your writing. Not a fickle goddess.

Never abandon the project. Just give it a little time off.

Over-scheduled?

Writer's Refusal may also occur when we have over-scheduled.

What we think is Writer's Block can be a sense of being overwhelmed.

Even God rested on the seventh day. Don't be a slave driver. Take a break—from that current project only. After all, we are creating, and six days of creation will sap our brains. Obey a writing Sabbath, on whichever day of the week works best for you. (After all, Saturday or Sunday as the Sabbath is merely an arbitrary human decision, much as the length of months is an arbitrary human decision.)

When you're overwhelmed because you're over-scheduled, then you need to schedule a break.

Break-away from Project 1 to work on Project 2. Take a couple of days or three or four to break ground for the next project. Do your research for Project 2. Sketch out ideas. Block out a series of scenes. Explore character development. Draw out a house plan. Or create a map with a free program, such as SmartDraw.

Or do some basic marketing drafts for Project 1. Marketing, by the way, is a separate project from writing the novel. Even though both are like conjoined twins, they require completely different thinking caps. Go ahead and write the blurb for the story. Figure out your tagline. Decide what your promotions are going to be.

Sometimes writing the blurb keeps you on track—and if you stray off, then you can always re-write the blurb to fit. Taglines need to capture the story in a catchy way. Call them one-sentence wonders. They make great ad copy and tweets.

Taglines require tight writing: 20 words or less. Whether on the cover or in an ad or both, taglines are just as important as the opening line and the opening scene of the book. They also require a bit of rhetorical savvy, either with climatic ordering or alliteration or clever metaphors, or some other rhetorical device. And they should give a quick glimpse of the story and spark the reader's interest.

For my book *Christmas with Death*, the tagline is "Christmas is for miracles, merriment, and murder." Readers know from the beginning that the book is a murder mystery. The alliterative M creates a bit of catchiness that will hopefully gain a second glance from the reader.

When I ran into a slump, I spent a day working on this tagline. Several hours that resulted in only seven words seems like an inefficient use of time; however, those seven words are the first ones that the reader will see. And as I continued writing *Christmas with Death*, I skipped back into the story to add scenes and situations to develop the ideas of miracles and merriment.

When the draft for Project 1 is ready for editing, you have your marketing decided.

Once you have completed Project 1 (and not just ended it), you can tranquilly turn to Project 2.

Sometimes, however, a simple break-away is not sufficient. Other break-aways are available.

Break-away from Genre. Writing the same type of thing, while it has equal measures of comfort and fit, doesn't always feed our brains. While marketing is different from writing, it doesn't really break away from Project 1.

That's when breaking away from the genre you're working in becomes a necessity.

One of the best ways to break-away from genre is to write something different from what you usually write. We spend our days working on our projects, composing emails, popping off tweets, and spewing out FB posts.

When you need a break-away from genre, you need to write something else. Whether you're writing fiction or non-fiction, break-away with a poem. A poem requires a completely different skill set. While you don't have to rhyme, you do need to create highly visual images. You compose in tight phrasings rather than long sentences.

Or write a journal. Follow the same instructions as for the Escape Exercise above, yet continue the writing for 30 minutes. Just let the writing flow freely, without considering structure or unity or coherence or even communication.

Freely-written and unstructured writing benefits the slavish novelist. If you're a poet, then write a story. This requires you to lengthen your thoughts and add in descriptions of characters and settings that you normally just touch upon. Compressing ideas into a compact poem helps the prose writer clarify ideas and tighten words. The lengthy exposition and narration of a story helps stretch out the poet's thought process, loosening it up before re-tightening.

Break-away from words completely if these escapes and first break-away options don't work.

How do you break-away from words? You work with numbers.

When you believe your creativity is zapped, turn to something totally analytical. Take an hour or two to set up a business ledger. Track month-by-month income/outgo report. You can call it Credits/Debits or Earnings/Expenses if you wish. Project expenditures into the future. What earnings are needed to fund those projected expenses? After totting up columns of numbers, the brain will beg to return to creativity.

Create a running tally, month to month, of the following items.

Office supplies: any writing tools, paper, printer ink/toner, paper clips, sticky notes and flags, binders, staples, stapler, three-hole punch, flash drives.

Mileage: You can use an app to record your miles, or you can keep a little notebook. Either way, check your trip-log against your planner to ensure that everything is added in. Note down the reason for the trip: research, inspiration, consultation, marketing, supply run, etc.

Operating Equipment: desktop or laptop, special software cost, internet access, any subscription programs (such as internet hosting or email aggregator like MailChimp or mileage tracker or computer planner), and inkjet or laser jet printer with scanning capability.

Operating Expenses: What do you have to have to be a writer, to promote your writing, and to publish your writing? To be a writer you need software (Scrivener, MS Word, Vellum). You also need developmental editors and content/line editors. To promote your writing, you need internet access and advertisements and swag (marketing materials). Publishing expenses include your cover designer, your agent (if you're traditionally published), and the printing cost of the book (if you're publishing it yourself or with a vanity publisher).

Professional expenses include any organizations to which you pay dues. Whatever your genre, you need to belong to a national organization which has as a primary purpose the defense of writers. These people are your professional tribe, brains with which you consult when you are thinking about the writing business.

Running all of these numbers will make the creative side of your brain wish it were working with words. And when tax time rolls around, you will pat yourself on the back.

And the result? Never lose sight of Apelles' mantra: *Nulla Dies Sine Linea*, but do escape or break-away from the current project.

How long should an escape or break-away last? One day? A week? A month? A season? However long it takes to become unburdened by the project.

Caveat ~ If we escape longer than a week, dive into another major project while letting the first one sleep.

We should let one project sleep while we work on another one. The combination of rest/work allows the subconscious to focus on Project One (P1) while the analytical conscious part of our brain works on Project Two (P2). When the subconscious engages, creativity thrives[31].

Plunge into the white-hot creative rush of Project Two. In a week, check on Project One. Brains that say "no" then will return to P2. Brains that say "yes" will return to P1.

Every day that we think about P1 while we work on P2 is a good sign. Our brain wants to take it back up. And our brains will tell us—sometimes with a shout—that it wants to return to P1. The "need" to return to it will seem overpowering.

Juggling two projects at once can be a good thing—especially for full-time writers who can build in a break: P1 in the A.M.; P2 in the P.M. after lunch and a walk.

When we beat Writer's Refusal, we've beaten that little gremlin that tried to control us and that multiplied exponentially. Just like the movie.

Writer's Procrastination

Writer's Procrastination is worse than simple Writer's Refusal, but it is also one that we should kick ourselves for having. This is a problem that we can control, just as we can control Refusal. Unlike the previous problem, however, it requires a change of our mindset. And your mindset can be a bug to change.

What has to change?

1st, while procrastination is defined as putting off something until a later time,

---

[31] This paragraph presents the focus of chapter 6.

you have to understand that true procrastination is not just delaying and delaying.

We delay things all the time. When we come home after a stressful day of work and say, "My brain is fried. I'll balance my bank account tomorrow." That delay means that we need a break, and we give in to it. We do get to the task we delay, usually within a couple of days.

Delay is also what a teen-ager does when he won't stop banging on the drums for the five minutes it will take to carry out the trash. That delay is a touch of rebellion.

True procrastination not only delays a project but delays it for so long that the deadline passes. We then blow through a second deadline. And even if we set a third deadline, we don't put impetus behind our work on a project.[32]

True procrastination is fear-driven. Yes, fear-driven. And we call it Writer's Block to keep from admitting our fears and confronting them. Confronting them is easy. Admitting them—it's been called half the battle. Our fears relate to the end result. If we didn't fear that result, we would grab the project and finish it in a timely manner.

How do we diagnose that we have procrastination? Did you take the quiz? Okay, maybe you need a few more examples.

- Do you have a closet filled with manuscripts that you've never shown anyone?
- Have you completed NaNoWriMo each year for the past seven years, but you've never gone back and fixed those manuscripts for publication?
- Have you reached the hard part of your story, jumped past to write other parts, and never come back to finish that hard part?
- Have you gotten excited about what you are writing only to lose that excitement a half-hour later because you remember someone saying it's not any good?
- Are you worried that your writing is not good enough because you want it

---

[32] If some outside force interferes with your writing time, preventing you to finish on your first, second or even third deadline AND you are still working steadily on the project, then procrastination is not your problem. You are not in a writing slump; you've got an outside force interfering. Call your problem what it is, then try to fix it. Some outside forces can't be fixed. If your income depends on an outside job that consumes your writing time (or your writing brain), then carefully weigh your short-term and long-term goals.
Do not take out a bank loan and a year off from work to pursue your writing dream. Be realistic, for heaven's sake.

to be perfect?

- Did you say you need to write but three hours later you're still a couch potato? And even more of a couch potato another hour after that?

While several bloggers have classified the writer's Top 3 Fears or 5 Worst Fears or the 10 Reasons for Writer's Block Defined, all of those listed fears actually boiled down to just two. Only two.

That should make them easy to overcome, shouldn't it? Nope.

Remember, I said confronting the fear is the easy part. Admitting them is half the battle. Admission is all about your perspective, your mindset. Admission is wanting a goal more than you want the fear.

When you admit your writing fear, then you can overcome it. And overcoming procrastination requires a change in your mindset. One small increment at a time.

We can change our mindset by setting deadlines and writing every day. Those two commitments—deadlines and *Nulla dies sine linea*—will help us keep our impetus as we pursue our goal of professionalism.

Any change to our mindset requires devotion. And Writer's Procrastination requires more devotion to overcome it. It's a real beast.

What are the two fears that drive true procrastination?

Fear of Failure

When we're working on a "heart" project, something near and dear to us, we may fear that no one will like—accept—what we have to say. Do we fear that no one will buy our writing?

Send that manuscript out to traditional publishers: A lucky few of us may be snapped up by editors. Most of us are star-crossed. We face rejection from the Trads. Never fear: Indie publishing awaits. When we do our job as writers to put the best product before the public, yet the Trads say, "not this time, but do try us again", then Indie publishing is the best route for us.

Defeating the fear of failure is simple: if one mountain implodes, find another one to climb. Creative people look for other options.

Only your definition of success matters. As long as we keep writing, we haven't failed. Re-define success into terms that you can control, not terms that are dependent on luck or on someone else's point of view.

After all, what is it you want to achieve? Money? Fame? Those are dependent on hard work and luck. You can't control luck.

Do you want to support yourself with your writing? That takes an investment of time, the several years necessary to complete several projects and reach the 20 or 30 books necessary for discoverability. If you remain devoted to your writing, that kind of success will come.

Do you want to reach out to others and influence them? Write truth in the best way that you know how. People respond to truth.

Your writing will speak to some people, and they'll buy it. If not many buy it, marketing may be the problem and not the ideas or the writing itself.

Spend your non-writing time looking for various ways to market the book. Yes, this is writing, just as creating and adhering to a Business Ledger is part of the writing business. Marketing and budgeting are not fun but are necessary. Be a Professional and handle the necessaries along with the fun.

Fear of Judgment

Criticism can be worse than fear of failure (rejection).

Let's distinguish between critiques and criticism. Well-intentioned critiques point out flaws. Criticism is people telling us their bad thoughts about our work.

Some traditional editors will write a critique with the rejection letter. Take these to heart; study them. When editors mention ways to improve our writing, we've managed a wonderful thing and touched some part of them. Well-intentioned critiques point out holes in the plot, faults with continuity, illogical actions and reactions of our characters, and info-dump (a serious crime). From friends and critique group members to reviewers, these critiques may seem harsh but are designed to improve the writing. Thank these people. They want to help you. They ARE helping you.

Criticism is different. Criticism denigrates without giving hope for improvement.

We have all heard horror stories of evil troll editors who reject with such comments as "your writing is atrocious" or "Never send us any more of your work". These are sad people who are interested only in spreading personal misery. Why else would they write something beyond the formula of "we're sorry, but this writing does not meet what we are looking for"? For those of us who have been burned, we may want to say "Writer's Block" when we actually should say, "evil troll editors".

Readers can become trolls. Wannabe writers who never accomplish anything can become trolls. The worst trolls are the fellow writers who are struggling with their own fears. You don't have to go far into writers' message boards before you will read about bad reviews, sabotage, and other icky behavior.

Dealing with Trolls

Some trolls delight in spreading their misery. They delight in causing pain. Edgar Allan Poe called such behavior "the imp of the perverse", the little demons inside us that enjoy creating painful problems for others.

These little demons may call themselves "tricksters," but they are nothing like Coyote of Native American myth. They have an evil appetite, like Loki of Norse myth, who has been classified as a trickster but is actually a shapeshifter, pretending to do good while actually working for evil.

These trolls—along with the ones who tell us they could write a better book but never have or the ones who tell us they figured out everything by page 20 of a 300-page book—delight in seeing our reactions.

For the ones who say they could write a better book—or they have a book idea they want to share with us so we can write it, as if we need more ideas— offer to be their First Reader when they finish the manuscript. Then walk away.

For the ones who tell us they figured out the ending or that "all romance novels are the same", ask them if they enjoy Bond movies or see a movie after they've read the book. Those endings are expected. Ask the reason that they stay for those movies. Listen to the answer. Hope they see the connection--comfort yourself when they do not see it. ;) And walk away.

For the shapeshifters, we must quietly remove them from our lives. Seriously. Do we want such two-faced people around us? They will suck creativity dry, and that may be the cause of our procrastination.

Evil trolls destroy hope. Avoid them.

Challenge the nay-sayers; tell them, "Watch me achieve my dream." And know that they are too afraid of their own dreams to pursue them.

Writer's Inertia

Inertia is the most insidious form of the so-called Writer's Block. This one is the true monster. A slimy monster of stagnation.

Inertia is "the tendency to do nothing, the tendency to remain unchanged." Oh, the two types of inertia—these are the real bad boys.

Wanting to Do Nothing ~ a Sign of Depression

Here are four healthy habits that can lift away lethargy and the doldrums.

1st, get sunshine. Get outside for 30 minutes per day. If it's cloudy, stay outside an extra fifteen minutes. In deep winter, increase that amount of time or take a Vitamin D plus K supplement. Give the supplement time to work.

The sunshine will have an effect within three days. Real sunshine is always better than a supplement, but if it's deep winter and you're in a northern latitude, get that D w/K supplement.

Getting your 30 minutes yet seeing no change?

2nd, cut sugar intake. Remember that starches (potatoes, rice, pasta, and breads) convert rapidly to sugar. Sugar gives a one-hour high then dumps you for four hours, at minimum.

Artificial and lab-made sugar is worse than cane sugar. At all costs, avoid high fructose corn syrup and the artificial sweeteners that raise blood sugar (and they all raise blood sugar. Don't believe the hype.).

You can have sugar, but you don't need to have it at every meal. And you don't need to snack.

Got sunshine? Cut sugar? After a week, still no change?

3rd, check your water intake. 64 oz. minimum. Make sure you drink filtered water. Pick one of the non-fluoridated forms: osmosis-filtered or distilled or spring water. I find water with electrolytes best of all. Notice: no carbonation, no energy drinks, no sugar, no fillers or other additives. Do not count your cup of coffee at breakfast or your glass of tea at lunch or your glass of wine at dinner. 64 ounces of water is in ADDITION to these other drinks.

If you need to flavor your water, then use organic citrus or fruits. The grated rind and slices of an organic lemon with filtered water poured over, this should be your go-to refreshment throughout the day. Mint tea is also good and wonderfully warming during cold weather. See that word "refreshment"? That's the point. Not a sugar high. Not a sweet incentive. Not a surge. Not bland. Water with citrus or mint re-charges you steadily.

Pay attention to your intake of water. Quality matters. Quantity matters. You should drink 32 ounces (a quart or a liter) within an hour of waking up. You've gotten dehydrated while you slept. You should try for another pint (16 ounces) by noon. Another pint by dinner leaves you with an extra cup or two before you go to sleep—and you're over your requirement, which is always good.

Yes, your bladder will send you running for the first week or so, but eventually it will learn the new schedule. Curiously enough, your body will realize hydration is now a regular thing and not hold on to the water at the cellular level. Drinking water when you don't feel well is hard; keep at it.

4th, walk for 30 minutes—slow or fast, doesn't matter. If you sweat—yes, sweat—add a minimum of one 8-ounce glass to your water intake for every 15 minutes of sweat-inducing exercises.

As you work at your desk or in a chair with laptop on your knees or on a little cart, get up every 25 minutes or so. Sitting too long is even more detrimental than exercise exhaustion. Work 25 sitting, break 10 for movement, repeat. Set a timer to keep you on track.

Movement is good for your body. If your back or neck has been bothering you, then moving your legs will work out those kinks. If you feel a little swollen or bloated or stuffed, the movement will move on out. Movement energizes the brain. Exhaustion doesn't. Don't push and push and push past endurance. You're not helping your body with such behavior. We are designed for movement, steady walking with occasional bursts of speed or energy.

Adding a daily walk when you haven't been walking will at first be wearying, but gradually the exercise gives you additional energy. You will need to walk on four opportunities at a steady 30 minutes before your body re-sets, so you need to give this one a week.

The wrong diet causes brain fog and sluggish memory. Fire that brain up with sun and water and exercise, and don't dumb it down with sugar. And the so-called Writer's Block from diet-& life-induced depression will dissipate[33].

---

[33] Diet-& life-induced depression is not clinical depression, which is caused by brain chemicals misfiring. This is not doldrums. Three signs of clinical depression—and I'm not a doctor—are feeling helpless, hopeless, and worthless. These feelings never

Remaining Unchanged—the Slime of Stagnation

Our world is one of constant change: the seasons, the days, the sky. We are also intended to change. Without it, we become stagnant. Without it, we can't shine.

Some may say their writing waits on inspiration. You never wait on inspiration; inspiration waits on you. It's ready to pour out at the opportune moment. And if you aren't actively seeking it, that opportune moment for inspiration will fly past.

Accept challenges. They help our minds to grow. Accept trials and grief. They help our souls to grow. As Clarissa Pinkola Estes says in her *Women who Run with the Wolves*, "Without death, there is no dark for the diamond to shine from."

Seek out change. Writers thrive on "what if?" "What if" is all about change. Change is all about improvement. Cast the net back into the world with the little worm of "what if" on the end. Break the mold of the same-old, same-old. Write new things. Try new things.

Visit museums. These are artists at work. Even if you don't like their paintings, even if you can't understand what the artist is trying to convey, study the composition. Look at how the colors are put together. Look at the shapes chosen and how the shapes are placed. Is the dominant image centered or off to one side? Which side? What individual elements besides the dominant image stand out? What is placed in the foreground? What is in the background?

Study the sculptures. Most of them will be modern. What is the artist trying to say? Why did s/he pick that form?

While driving down a street, look at the buildings. How are they distinguished from the others? Is it the paint alone, or are there differences in the brick construction? What old buildings need to be revived? What brand-new buildings need to be razed? Why? Why?

---

lift. If you lack the energy even to think about making changes, if you feel the shadow of doom constantly hanging over you, and if you think no one cares for you and nothing matters in your life, YOU ARE WRONG. Please get some kind of help. You matter. Even if I don't know you, I will tell you that you matter. Everyone who is here on Earth has a purpose in life, and you have a fulfilling purpose that will make you happy. You just need to find it.

Take a hike. Leave the mall and walk through a park. Go to a local garden store and browse through the flowers and trees and learn more than the names of the ones that appeal to you. Introduce yourself to the infinite variety of trees and shrubs and flowers, perennials and annuals.

Go to a symphony—or listen to one. Pick something you would not usually like. Read the liner notes before you listen. Pay attention to the musicians working together to create this music. Consider the style, the use of volume. Watch the conductor and her/his use of energy while directing. And if you've never been to a symphony before, wait for others to clap before you do. (There are brief pauses between major movements in symphonic compositions. Don't applaud a movement; only applaud a symphony.)

Go to a local theater. Stroll through a gallery. Visit a little shop; you don't have to buy. Spend 30 minutes there rather than in front of the TV or buried in your phone.

Learn the names of the common birds you see. That's a cardinal, not a red bird. That's a robin hopping along, a chickadee swooping, a little wren putting all the effort in his tiny body to sing the loudest song in your backyard.

Learn new things constantly. Try new things constantly. Go to new local places. Stretch out.

And think WHY. Why is it this way? Why do I like it? Why don't I like it? How would I change it?

Wrapping Up

Remember, we're going Pro. Remember deadlines. Remember our mantra ~ *Nulla Dies Sine Linea*. Now add this injunction: *Writer's Block doesn't exist.* Never say or write or think that two-word phrase again.

Be a three-souled writer: Heed your heart's desire. Apply your gut to the work. Think through problems to defeat them.

What escape do you need to plan for?

What fear do you need to cast out?

What change do you need to seek out?

Ask these three questions, and get back to writing.

Chapter 6 ~ One Slice of Advice :: Let it Sleep

Writing projects flow through the seasons of the year, including the dormancy of winter.

Every year hurries into spring, blooming and leafing into growth. Summer thrives greenly, burning through the long days until we are finished with the heat and are longing for chill mornings and temperate days. We yearn for the blazing colors of autumn.

In winter the land rests, dormant after three busy, busy seasons of sprouting, growing, and fruiting.

Nature needs winter, her time to re-gather her resources as the fields lie fallow and nutrients gently decay into the rich soil to nourish later plantings.

Writers hurry into projects, creating and crafting stories and blogs into growth. We thrive on generating ideas to develop those blossomed stories, and we burn through projects as we sketch and draft and revise until our projects reach fruition.

Just like Nature, writers need to let their projects lay dormant a season before being reborn as a published work.

We need to allow some projects the time to be buried, as Winter buries the land in cold snow before the Spring sun warms it back up.

Let It Sleep

I have advised you to set and keep deadlines. I want you to have *Nulla Dies Sine Linea* as your mantra. I've spoken heresy by preaching *Writer's Block Doesn't Exist* and by counseling you to write something, even if it's not what you are working on.

Yet now I am saying to let a project "sleep". Am I now talking out of both sides of my keyboard? Am I contradicting myself?

No.

This is talking about projects. After the seasons of creating and drafting and revising, we need to let the project sleep. Close it up, cover it over with another project. Walk away for a time.

"But it's finished!" you protest. Is it?

The benefit comes in the creative process. The conscious mind may have cast the project from immediate contemplation. The subconscious, however, continues to filter in new resources. That happened with this very manual. It's the reason this is the *revised* edition.

Save your final edit for after the project's dormant season. When editing begins, new ideas may surface that will enrich the project in ways you did not fathom as you designed and drafted then blazed through the revision. Here's the reason ~

Sleeping awakens the dreaming creativity.

I have urged that we should not wait on inspiration. Inspiration waits on us. It lurks, waiting to spring out at opportune moments. It will plant itself where it belongs. As it grows, like honeysuckle, inspiration may reach into unexpected and unwanted areas. It may require gutting and inserting, reworking and re-sequencing the original.

Acquaint yourself with the work of Tony Buzan. Buzan explores the realm of creativity. He coined the term "mind-mapping" for a particular style of idea exploration.

Mind-mapping and similar explorations come into play not just at the start of a project but also after any season of dormancy. Many writers have created collages as inspiring guides for a project. The collage or mind-map can be just as useful when re-approaching a supposedly finished project after its winter sleep.

Letting ideas flow out without any editor (the hardest part of our brain to turn off) will create the dream-like state in which creativity thrives. Follow the growth of inspiration, and the transformed project will be so much better. You will no longer begrudge the laborious hours birthing and nurturing, pruning and training to meld the new work with the old.

Whether you decide to launch into the next project or whether you decide to spend some dreaming time with this project, you need to kindle the right side of your brain to awaken creativity.

13 Ways to Spark Creativity

Tilt your head sideways ~ 1.

This means to think unconventionally. Look for unusual connections.

Play a game to find different ways to match up things that aren't normally match-able. Ink becomes tattoos become hieroglyphs become spiderwebs.

Another form of this is to transform the use of a common object. For example, turn a brick into a bird feeder or a pencil holder or a kitchen trivet for a hot pot.

Mind Maps and Free-writing ~ 2.

Both processes follow where the brain leads. Do both with pen/cil and paper, not on computer. Using the hand awakens the brain. Drs. Carrie and Aaron Barron discuss this in their book *The Creativity Cure*.

Tony Buzan has several videos on youtube as well as books that describe Mind Maps. The visual flow of words is an open cluster-form to which is added color (which pleases the brain). Use flowing, curving lines and circles rather than straight, blocky lines and squares. Don't edit; follow the brain's path, not your own.

Embrace absurdity in this exercise, the type of absurdity that Lewis Carroll, Monty Python, Salvador Dali, and Marx Brothers are known for.

Dream Writing ~ 3.

You've heard this one before, I know. Write down your dreams as soon as you awaken. Don't try to make sense of what you are writing; just write. Jot down what you remember. A form of this is the escape exercise in the previous chapter.

Don't strive for complete sentences. Phrases and single words work just as well. Come back after a few hours and turn these notes as well as any other surfaced ideas into a journal.

Avoid perfection. You are capturing ideas and broad plans. When you dip back into the writing (or cycle back in), you can develop the ideas and plans and expand the scene with details. And if you aren't keeping a writing journal for random ideas and mind maps and dreams, start now.

Dream writing is the system used when doing Writing Sprints (Chris Fox's *5,000 Words per Hour*) and Cycling (Dean Wesley Smith and his *Writing Into the Dark*). After the sprint cycle back into the writing for improvements, development, and enhancements.

30 Circles Exercise ~ 4.

Bob McKim of the Stanford Design Program developed this creativity exercise. Draw 30 circles of equal size on a page. (I'll let you use a computer for only the drawing portion of the exercise. Use the print-out for the actual exercise). Set a timer for three minutes. In each of the circles, draw recognizable objects of any sort. The items don't have to match. Have fun. Be silly.

Scenarios from Observation ~ 5.

Go to a public space. Select a single person walking past, and write down 10 observable facts. Use those facts to determine their emotional state, the background to this state, and what actions they will take next.

Switch Genres ~ 6.

I also discussed a form of this exercise in the last chapter. This time, however, turn a story into a poem, a non-fiction self-help blog into a rap song. Or write a story to the movements of a musical composition (such as Strauss' "Thunder and Lightning Polka").

Moving from music to words is a switch-up called translating by John Ingledew in *How to Have Great Ideas: A Guide to Creative Thinking*. He has described how Wassily Kandinsky used classical music to inspire his abstract paintings (music to brushstrokes).

If you don't wish to switch genres—that is, switching will make you kick and scream—then try out the story challenge from Ernest Hemingway[34]: write a

---

[34] Hemingway is often credited, although Wikipedia says that similar challenges

story in 6 words. Here's his: For sale: baby shoes, never worn.

7 in 7 ~ 7.

Over seven days, draw seven different objects: coffee cup, apple, lamp, koi, etc. Add as much detail as you wish, but don't try to be exact. Loose-form drawing is better. Avoid stick figures in this exercise.

Knolling ~ 8

Knolling is lining up similar types of items in an organizational juxtaposition. Now, while in # 7 loose-form sketches were better, for knolling you will have rigid organization. The difference is that you are not writing or sketching; you are placing items. The rigid organization that requires the analytical left brain frees up the right brain for creative thoughts while you work.

Group similar tools in parallel and/or perpendicular ways. Find a way to match up seemingly dissimilar items. Pens and pencils are similar; place three forms of rulers beside them.

You can use your office supplies, utensils in a kitchen drawer, make-up supplies, and tools from the household tool box. Anything that has items for a similar use can be knolled.

Of course, don't forget to put everything back in place.

Sleep on It ~ 9.

This is not #3. Write down a problem right before you go to sleep. This should be the last thing you do before you turn out the light. If you have a work issue or a sticky issue in a story, write it down. When you wake, your brain may have given you an answer, likely in symbols.

Collage ~ 10

Create a collage for each of your primary characters (protagonists and antagonists). Work on one character at a time. Don't edit. If you see an image that strikes you as interesting and fitting, cut it out and paste it on.

---

predate him. This exercise is often called Flash Fiction.

This may take days. Old magazines work very well. Your Pinterest feed may have interesting images to use; screenshot and print them out before cutting them out in different ways. You can use stock photos as well. Don't look for specific images; just browse what's newest or generic collections.

You can also take a series of photos when in a public place. People, objects, plants, cars, buildings, sidewalks, everything is literal and figurative fodder for your creative brain.

Storyboard ~ 11

Time for stick figures. Tell your story through a series of panels similar to comic-book blocks. You may use stick figures and basic representations of items. You can be detailed.

You can write captions for each panel. Characters can speak in bubbles and have light-bulb moments.

Six Thinking Hats ~ 12

Edward de Bono in his 1985 book of the same title recorded these ideas.

Work a primary character through each of these decision-making processes.

Logic ~ facts only, neutral and objective, cold

Optimism (rose-colored glasses) ~ positives and plus points, an idea's usefulness

Devil's Advocate (or Judge) ~ cautionary, the worst that can happen, spotting difficulties and dangers

Emotion ~ feelings, gut reactions, fears and wishes

Creativity ~ possibilities, alternatives, inventiveness, elaboration

Management ~ direction, organization, synthesis, metacognition

Awaken the Brain ~ 13.

Listen to music, dance, do slow-moving exercises like Tai Chi and flexibility/yoga, meditative coloring, working with blues and greens in pencils or markers or paint ~ all of these increase creativity.

While It Sleeps

Creativity relies upon the suppression of the active Left Brain in order to let the subconscious Right Brain speak to us, through symbols, images.

As you can engage in the thirteen exercises as daily activities, one a day over two weeks, you also need to look for other things to do to keep your hands off the project you are letting sleep.

On farms, winter is the season used as preparation for the approaching growing season. During the cold months, when the Earth lies dormant, farmers look over their fences and barns and sheds, over their equipment and their records of previous years, and over their livestock and seed hoards. They are engaged in repairs, restocking, and re-considering. What should we writers do while our projects are sleeping?

Repairs

Look for a project that you abandoned because it wasn't quite working.

Re-acquaint yourself with that project's concept then work through a mind-map or collage or a similar creative tool. This is in addition to the other creative activity you are doing on that day. The season of sleep for this abandoned project may have given your subconscious time to work out the corner you wrote yourself into.

Did it have a Damocles' sword hanging over it, something that distracted you from the project's fruition so that you just could not focus on where you were in the project? Perhaps after that season of sleep, you can discern the sword of Damocles that interfered with your project's completion. You must do that analysis in order to determine what cut through your focus by dangling overhead.

Or pick up the next project you're contemplating. Do its research. Determine the lodestone that will keep you returning as it develops from planting to growing to harvest.

Restocking

While pursuing a project's completion, we all have a stray idea or two or three that wanders through our minds. We make a note of it then continue on with our primary focus.

Many writers keep an ideas journal. In down-times I peruse it. What can I use now? What can still wait? Which idea's time has come? During the project's dormancy, return to these stray ideas and give them a home.

Which ideas spark more and start to develop into a story? Which ideas still must wait? Which idea's time has come to turn into a project?

Sketch out a chosen few of these ideas or even take them to the outline step. Map out their start to finish, then decide how to fit them into your schedule of upcoming projects. Those newly-homed strays are not yet a project, however. Set them aside. The time for their planting will come.

Re-considering

During the primary project's Winter, take a look at this writing business you are pursuing. It is a business, right? No longer a hobby or escape, but something you are pursuing for income?

Is the business seeing growth? Or do you seem to be digging into the same infertile ground?

TRACK the $$

Do a cost analysis. You should see a return on the money you've put into the business. If you're not earning (making a little more year to year), what do you need to change? Marketing? More blogging? More freelance work?

Where were you profligate with your writing expenses? Where did you waste $$? I cannot resist charming little journals. Yes, I am a paper nut, for I have over a dozen now with no immediate opportunity for their use. I am a pen nut, too.

Our profligate expenses may be in paying others to do things that we could have figured out on our own. However, sometimes it behooves us to pay others to do those things IF we spend that time saved in writing. If that time saved was not put to writing . . . well, what a waste.

TRACK the DAYS

Count the days during the year when you actually wrote, and analyze what happened on your unfruitful days. What time did you waste?

Another time-expense occurs with our relationships. We do need to devote time (and money) to family and friends. Humans are social creatures. Just look at the most introverted people you know when they are placed with people they love, talking about something they feel in their heart: they become gregarious.

Driving to and from major family gatherings is not a waste of time. For these gatherings, if you feel you *must* write, you can always dictate into your phone. If you're with others while driving and can't dictate and can't write in the backseat because you're the driver, how can you use this time? Talk to them about movies: the characters, the plot, the setting. You are getting a layman's view of story. A truly helpful passenger will write down anything you dictate . . . and could brainstorm ideas as well.

TRACK your ENERGY

Time and Money are not the only elements of your Cost Analysis. Are you properly using your writing energies? Refer back to the "Writer's Block" chapter, specifically in the area of Writer's Inertia.

What things energize you? We all have moments when everything flows out, clear and clean as a mountain stream, rushing so quickly we can barely get the words down. These moments are to be celebrated.

We also have moments when we feel totally drained. Creative writing is difficult at such moments. We don't have to lose those moments. By keeping works in various stages of progress, we can edit and correct even if we can't really "write".

In addition, we have moments when we just have to grind out the words. They lack fire, but we need to get them down.

Writing can sometimes be more grunt-work that fired-work. Acknowledging the adage that "Writers re-write" becomes a boon. We know—and can make notes—that this scene just isn't right, not yet, but it will become better.

This grunt writing is one of those times when we can record the problem before we go to sleep. Our subconscious will work on the problem and present the answer the next morning or during the next day.

The End of the Season of Sleep

Unlike the vernal equinox, we may not have a demarcation to help us know when the winter of our project is over. Such a winter does not have a set number of days. The return to your project will not have a set timeline.

When you have repaired and restocked and re-considered and researched, you should feel a sense of completion, just as the land does not wait upon the equinox. If you do not feel that sense of completion, then move to another project. Leave the other sitting, steeping, becoming richer in your mind.

We are not developing products on a factory system. We are artists who happen to be authors. We aren't waiting on the muse; we are writing other projects until the creative impulse for the first project returns.

Sometimes Spring is reborn early; sometimes it is late. One day that first project will warm up in your mind. Give it first frost, perhaps even a second, then you can plant ink into the editing process.

Even when you fly through with few changes, you have lost nothing to the winter season. When you finish this project, you have another waiting, ready to start or in the beginning stages. Your mind can turn to it because it has let go of the first project. You didn't just end it; you completed it.

That strong sense of closure can only be attained if your project has its dormancy and then re-awakening.

Let it sleep.

Chapter 7 ~ One Resolution :: Be a Writer

Be Resolved.

The first of the year is traditionally the time to reflect over the past year and consider the upcoming year. Everyone creates a list of resolutions for the coming year.

For my writing resolutions, I never can wait for January 1st—or even December 31st. The holidays have so many distractions that I want my coming year planned long before the first day of the New Year.

Typically, I do the thinking part of my reflection throughout the month of November. After Thanksgiving, on the first Sunday of the Advent Season when I am appropriately grateful for all I've received, I create a written plan for the next year using a calendar, generating a series of deadlines for my writing from the beginning of the year to the end.

The deadlines that are more than seven months in advance are more nebulous than tangible reality, but I find it helps to have a basic idea of where I want to go with my writing. It does help to have a Wish List.

This year-in-advance plan, set rolling, encounters disruptions before the end of the second season. I keep firming it up: the wishes that will become reality, the wishes that need to percolate longer, the wishes that have a little more consideration, and the wishes that might manage to crowd in.

By the start of September (eleven months after the initial plan), I know how much more I will be able to accomplish in the remaining four months of the year. Re-planning starts with the next Advent season.

The first day of Spring is another good choice for reflection and planning. Spring is rebirth and renewal, the beginning sprigs of new growth shooting up from the newly warmed ground. Spring is an excellent time to re-think your writing life and plant your plans for your writing year.

Other writers wait for the blazing heat of Summer to shine the light on their writing. Conditioned by many years of traditional public schools, they view May as an ending. June becomes an opportunity to re-launch, to burn out the interferences with their writing.

Whichever time of the year that you select: Advent or New Year's or Spring or Summer or even any other time of the year, Be Resolved.

Juggling

Set a plan for your projects. Consider how long they will take. Track the days; track the effort. Plan for your expenses several months in advance, and you will have the money needed when the time comes for publishing.

Keep one project at the fore. Focusing on it creates a steady pattern of work.

Keep another project advanced on the burner, turning to it when you do hit those draining lags. It may be at the research or character development or scene blocking stage. It may be in its Winter, waiting for a final proof.

Keep a third project at the simmer stage, making notes occasionally as the mood strikes.

If you can juggle four projects—one in focus, another at the research stage, a third waiting for proof, and a fourth merely simmering—go for it. I can juggle for a little while. At some point, one of the balls gets dropped. When I become intent on finishing the focus project, I become laser-sharp on that one.

Notice: I didn't say completing the focus project. Remember from last chapter? We need to give ourselves a little objective distance from what we think is finished before we call it completed. Set it on the back burner, and let it simmer a little while.

With other projects already in motion, we can easily pick them up and keep working, accomplishing more and more of our goals for the year.

When we move from finishing projects to completing them, we need to celebrate. Now is the time to tell others what we have accomplished.

Mantras

Somewhere, I think it was Pinterest, I came across the following: uncredited and totally anonymous but absolutely genius. You can find various versions, most a little more foul-mouthed, which people tend to like.

Set Goals. Don't Tell Anyone. Smash the hell out of them. Clap for your own damn self. Repeat.

I quibble with only one part of that: the "clap for your own damn self."

When we celebrate the completion of a project (not just finishing, remember?), we need to let people know. If you've completed a manuscript and you've followed Robert Heinlein's advice and put it on the market (whether by sending to a publishing house or an agent or by publishing it yourself), then celebrate with family and friends.

That celebration gives us something to anticipate as we grind through the drain-times of the next project.

Completion of projects and celebrating that completion will energize us as we enter the next project. No longer do we feel like Sisyphus, rolling an impossible boulder up an impossibly steep mountain. We know we can do it.

We've done it. We can do it again.

Set Goals. Long-term. Short-term. Achievable projects projected into the future. With deadlines.

Don't tell anyone. Not anyone. No matter how much you want to share a brilliant idea, wait until the project is completed. Don't lose the fire by sharing and having others nix it.

Smash the hell out of them. This may take months. Commitments might turn those months into years. We just keep advancing. Tracking our days. Knocking out the scenes, one at a time. Turning scenes into chapters and chapters into books. Getting it done.

Celebrate.

Repeat.

The # 1 Resolution

Here is your Resolution: I will *Think like a Pro*.

Author, poet, blogger, dramatist: all writers should have the same thought: I am a writer. That's the mind-set you snatch up and ingest. It must become part of your DNA, mutating through your being like a beneficial virus.

How do we change our view of our writing from mere hobby or escape to profession? Take three actions.

Be Devoted

"Thou shalt have no other gods before me," the commandment requires. This doesn't mean that other gods ($$$, celebrity, bling, shopping, gossip, salacious viewing, etc.) aren't out there; it means that nothing else comes before God.

We need to view writing with the same eagle-eyed focus. Be Devoted to writing. Don't worship it, yet don't let petty distractions and time wasters get between you and your pursuit of writing professionally.

How can we be devoted? By keeping our workspace professional.

❧ Turn off the distractions: the Boob Tube, Solitaire or Mahjongg, social media in whatever iteration currently distracts you, and email.

❧ Do you really need to watch every minute of the news or that reality show or house-flipping or endlessly running TV series and movie marathons? Have you noticed most of those shows repeat?

❧ Do you really need to post that cupcake to Pinterest? Do you need to see every image of cupcake? Why are you even looking at cupcakes?

❧ The twit who's tweeting you can wait. Help him learn patience.

❧ Nor do you need to respond instantly to emails. "But-but-my email?" you protest. Turn it off. You can answer anything that came in while you were writing *after* you finish the writing for the day.

❧ Social media has its place—for marketing your work. Make an appointment with yourself—once or twice a month or once a week—to spend the necessary promotional time on FB or Twitter or Pinterest and others.

❧ By the way, FOOD is also a distraction. Clean out the candy, popcorn, chips, the incessant mugs of coffee, and the sweet drinks. None of that is helping your brain. They start up sweet cravings (and remember that starches turn into sweets). Giving into those cravings merely sets off a ticking bomb for a system-depressor that will implode in about an hour. We need to write, not stare at the screen or blank paper because our brains are befogged. If eating is essential, carrots and sliced cucumbers and apples will give the body what it needs and can use.

Basically, anything that interferes with the work of writing goes away.

PARENTS may have to squeeze writing time into their day: get up earlier or stay up later. Write sitting on the bleachers. Sneak ideas into a journal in 10-minute or 20-minute increments. Make the SIGNIFICANT OTHER pull equal weight with household chores. By the way, the house doesn't have to be spotless. Ironing is not a necessity, but clean clothes are. Rinse the dishes as you use them; wash them every other day or slide them into the dishwasher.

Be Professional

To think like a professional, observe professionals.

❧ In Behavior ~ Observe professionals at the organizations they attend.

Distinguish among the people who attend these meetings: Pro, GonnaBe, Wannabe, and Newbie. A GonnaBe is on the path toward publication. A Wannabe is someone who claims to write but never actually does. If writing occurs, s/he never actually finishes. A Newbie has just started. Remember, completing a project is BIG. Some Wannabes and Newbies never reach this step.

Only occasionally will the Pros come out of the woodwork, primarily for seminars and special events (more about this behavior below). They will teach at these seminars; listen to them.

Those of us who have been writing for years can spot the problematic conference-attenders. These are the hobbyists and escapists who ask obvious questions. We cringe for them. They don't cringe. They don't even know they should be cringing. (Rant over.)

Pay the dues to belong. Writing organizations are helpful for introducing you to ideas you will not find on your own. Fellow members can give guidance and serve as mentors. They will also give you a sense that you are not collapsing, that your dream is transitioning to reality, and that you are not alone in your struggles.

Being a Pro also means giving back. Contribute where you can. Give advice only when it's asked for. Be helpful, not overbearing. The people you counsel and critique may become your audience.

The local writers' group may have two or three active professionals (pursuing writing and getting paid for it—even if only in small increments), so join it. If it has no professionals, then drive the distance necessary to get to an organization with active professionals.

❧ In Business

Professionals keep business and personal accounts separate. Hobbyists and escapists funnel everything through their personal accounts.

Separate financial accounts. If the writing $$ can't support a separate account, at least keep a ledger to track financials separately.

Separate your email accounts: apps abound that amass all email accounts into one place. When you reply, the reply leaves the app as if it's coming from the email it was directed to.

Tax Tips for Writers

Keep an accounting of your income & outgo (otherwise known as earnings & expenses or credits & debits).

We become so excited when we see our earnings; however, if you just place them into your regular monies, then you will never understand just how much you are actually earning. Keep a close track of that amount.

Also, keep a close track of the amount that you spend toward this hobby that's becoming a profession. Much of that amount, based on percentages, can be counted as deductions on your taxes.

Here is a rough list of items that you can count toward your taxes, as well as the categories to place them in. The key is that these items are devoted to writing, or only a percentage of them is allowed.

Office Supplies

Writing ~ pens/pencils, printer paper, writing paper, planner / journal, printer ink/toner

Grouping ~ paper clips, sticky notes and flags, highlighters, staples, stapler

Organization ~ binders, three-hole punch, file folders, file folder organization system (filing cabinet or smaller file folder holders)

Don't forget ~ flash drives and other physical items that you find necessary for writing and developing stories.

Office Equipment

Desktop/laptop, keyboard, mouse, mouse pad, task lamp

inkjet/laserjet printer with scanner

specialized software programs (whether MS Word or Scrivener or Vellum) internet access

for audio books: any special software programs, headphones/microphone, cost of reader, etc.

any subscription programs (such as internet hosting or email aggregator like MailChimp or mileage tracker or computer planner)

and any equipment rentals.

Operating Expenses

Beyond office supplies and office equipment, what do you have to have to be a writer, to promote your writing, and to publish your writing?

Do you have a separate bank account for your writing? The cost of that account should be deductible.

If you use your smartphone to write, to record mileage, to contact and consult your designers and editors, or for any use, then a percentage of its cost can be deducted. An accountant can tell you how much can be deducted and how to record its use in order to receive the deduction.

Business licenses and permits. To publish on electronic distributors like Amazon and Smashwords, you need a Tax Id number. That's a business license. ISBNs have to be purchased. The copyright fee has to be paid.

Publishing expenses include your cover designer, your agent (if you're traditionally published), and the printing cost of the book (if you're publishing it yourself or with a vanity publisher).

Do you have an email list aggregator like MailChimp or Drip, GetResponse, aWeber or ConstantContact? That's a cost.

If you are selling from your website, any fees that you pay to services like PayPal or Square should be counted. These count as Merchant Processing fees.

Also, if you are selling personally, you will need to collect sales tax and turn over any monies owed (taxes) to the proper authorities.

Measure out the size of your devoted writing space. (And this needs to be a devoted writing space.) . A percentage of your mortgage, based on the percentage of the writing space in relation to the size of the house, can be deducted. If an auditor walks through (God forbid) or that complaining skeptical aunt demands a tour of where you live, when you pass your writing space, you can point and say, "This is where I write."

Your writing space should look like a writing space. If it's a craft table pushed against the wall with the printer underneath, a small desk tucked into a closet, the bonus room above the garage that's half-filled with junk, or a study (lucky you), measure the size and report it on your tax form. If you rent an office (oh my, I am envious), then that cost counts.

Professional Expenses

Dues for any writing organization. Whatever your genre, you need to belong to a national organization which has as a primary purpose the defense of writers. Some organizations are genre-specific, such as Romance Writers of America and Science Fiction Writers of America, and the Mystery Writers of America, yet their advice and support will help you no matter which genre you write in—and even if your writing is not genre-specific.

Many of these organizations have different levels of membership—Guppies, in Sisters in Crime, is geared to the newbie writer. Some organizations are exclusive (Novelists Inc / NINC). Prowl around, and pay attention to events in the writing world, not just in your genre.

Do you have developmental editors and content/line editors? These go with any other consultation costs that you might have.

Have you purchased advertisements and swag (marketing materials)? Any cost that you have related to promotion, be certain to record it.

Seminars, conferences, continuing education classes, writing books: all of these show that you are attempting to improve your professional skill level.

- Classes & books show that you are improving your professional skill level. Keep the receipts.
- Conferences and seminars are opportunities for networking with other professional writers.
- Reader-specific conferences help you connect with your audience. Everything you do, marketing AND writing, is directed toward your readers. Interaction with them shows that you are building a market for your writing.

Professional gifts given, including meals and entertainment as well as tickets and other gifts. You are creating good will with the people that you contract with.

Mileage

You can use an app to record your miles, or you can keep a little notebook. Either way, check your trip-log against your planner to ensure that everything is added in.

Note down the reason for the trip: research, inspiration, consultation, marketing, supply run, etc.

Any auto expenses related to your work performance should also be counted. (I guess this means that, if you had a flat tire while driving to a conference, a *percentage* of that cost can be deducted. An accountant can give you more information.)

Miscellaneous Expenses

The cost of tax preparation

A percentage of your utilities (water, gas, electric), based on the size of your writing space.

Any other expenses specific to the writing industry

Some repairs and maintenance costs can be deducted. If they are related to writing, record them. Record as well the reason that these costs are related to your writing.

❧ In Focus

The reason many professionals only occasionally emerge at an organization's meeting is that they are writing. We need to be writing, too. So ask, "Do I need to attend *this* meeting?" Now this is a balancing act: supporting an organization takes time away from writing, but you need to support the organization.

However, your focus should be on the writing. This focus should include the people who see the first "public" version. Hobbyists and escapists have friends as First Readers (aka Beta Readers). These friends gush about how great the writing is. Nope. These are NOT the first readers that you need.

Before I talk about the readers you do need, **one word**: Be nice to all of your Beta Readers. Please don't give them the beta version. Beta developed as a term for *software that still had a lot of known bugs*; give your Beta Readers a polished manuscript (MS), not one with bugs you know about.

While professionals want to hear the MS is great, they would rather their Beta Readers were "mean" about the manuscript. Critique partners should look for

~~

- Plot holes

- Character dynamics
- Character synergy
- Continuity
- Info Dump
- Lack of Suspense / Pacing

Critique partners and Beta readers should mark all errors they see.

When they hand the MS back, be grateful and acknowledge their assistance in your published MS.

If it's the critique you need, you may want to cry or scream or burn it or all three at once. Avoid the last. And learn from the mistakes they found as you correct them.

Be Intrigued

One of the hardest parts of any professional career is maintaining a high interest level. The Resolution to BE a WRITER is hardest at this point.

Writing is the most difficult of jobs, primarily for its very isolation. Humans come with two wires: amiability and curiosity.

Family, friends, colleagues, and organizations both social and professional charge up our amiability wire. Keeping our curiosity charged is not so easy.

New projects entice us, yet before long our piqued interest fades. How can we maintain our curiosity when we know our characters and the plot and the setting and the outcome and the twists?

When a MS is getting you down, take a break from it. Add in a new character—or a new twist or new invention. Try something new. Tinker with it whenever the primary project is driving you crazy or deadening your senses.

And stay physically active. It is amazing how much physical activity drives intellectual activity. Move the body; energize the brain.

Finally, Being a Professional means that some days we just have to slog through the mud and grind the work out. That's okay. We can always re-write it.

After all, we're writers.

Closing

Overcoming difficulties is a constant process, no matter which profession you enter.

All the things that I have written in this little manual are insights that I wish someone had shared when I first started out. And I wish that someone had kept preaching these lessons to me. For most of these lessons, I was sitting in the choir. I knew them. I just didn't follow them.

I especially needed the lessons on *Nulla dies sine linea* and deadlines. Deciding to follow those two points alone finally put the wheels on my dream so I could travel the road to first publication and beyond.

I taught plot structures and character essentials for years before I realized— idiot that I was—hey, this relates to my own writing. I've said before: I'm not the brightest bulb, but I can still shine.

The lesson that Writer's Block Doesn't Exist took me *years* to learn. I told myself the lie of Writer's Block so many times. Then I willfully blinded myself because I wouldn't let my composition students use that lie.

I do remember the first time that I realized my students' so-called block was procrastination, and their procrastination was fear of failure. And I remember helping them realize that planning eased the path to completing their essays. I introduced them to clustering and avoided strict outlining for many, many years—then I eventually had to back up and ensure they understood outlining, a lesson on easing the planning path that was as important for me as it was for them. Mind maps and dream-type writing put the fun back into writing.

I had some overwhelming years with my job—especially while pursuing my Master of Arts in English degree. I continued to dabble at writing, using it as an escape, a time filler. I played at being a writer. I should have known better. At this point I realized the insidious difficulties of Writer's Refusal. I didn't call it that, but I certainly had time to write and didn't want to write.

Gradually I learned that putting bum in chair and running a writing sprint is a quick way over that hurdle.

And then came the dark years. About nine years before I set off on my journey to publication[35], I found myself wallowing in the slime of Writer's Inertia.

I didn't land in Inertia by choice. Part of it was depression from an overwhelming obligation for which I could see no way out. Part of it was issues with my thyroid. A third part of my inertia was a general hopelessness about writing. The road to publication through traditional publishing houses seemed closed.

I've written stories of some type since 4th grade. If I'm not writing bits and pieces that could turn into a story, I'm not happy. And the wallowing world of Inertia plopped me down into poisonous green slime. I couldn't see a way out.

Nevertheless, through the grace of loved ones who threw me a rope, I clutched at that lifeline and started pulling myself out.

Getting my thyroid straightened out fixed some of the inertia. The overwhelming obligation, however, wasn't going to lift any time soon. To escape it, rather than plop myself before the TV for yet more mindlessness, I returned to writing. Before I knew it, my nightly hour-long scribbles were turning into a story (thank you, God). I finished that novel and started another one.

My obligations became easier to deal with, but it took five more years before the leech of Inertia stopped sucking at my creative energies.

My looking up and seeing the sunshine again coincided with a drive to help my students become more creative. I had previously dissed some of the exercises in the 13 Ways to Spark Creativity. I dissed them before I tried them with my students. I was wrong.

When I no longer needed an escape, I returned to that God-gifted novel and revised it. I wrote another book. And another one (which you can find under my Remi Black pseudonym). I decided to finish the second novel. I started a second Remi Black. Finished it. Finished the other second novel. Thought about a third fantasy. Started a third Hearts in Hazard.

Then stopped.

---

[35] the journey described in the introduction. As of this writing, that would be about 14 years ago

Because I still felt hopeless about publication.

And then Amazon's Kindle revolutionized the book industry.

I came late to the Kindle revolution. I am extremely grateful to the indie writers who paved the way.

I looked at those writers and thought "Wow. I wish."

"If wishes were horses," the old proverb says, "beggars would ride." Took me about a year to figure that one out.

I know. I might shine, but I'm not the brightest bulb. I wish.

Wishing to be a published writer finally, finally clicked in my head with the Kindle revolution.

I had books. I needed a plan. And I won't repeat the plan ~ It's in the introduction. ;)

But of all the lessons in this little manual, it's the one in Chapter 7 that sticks with me.

One Resolution: Be a Writer. Be devoted. Be professional. Be intrigued.

And my mantra: Set goals. Don't tell anyone. Smash the hell out of them. Celebrate. Repeat.

I hope you take the 7 lessons of *Think like a Pro* and create your own *New Advent* as a writer.

Apply the lessons in any order that you wish. Soon, you will no longer view writing as a hobby. You will view it as the rewarding career that it is.

Think like a Pro. Soon, you *are* the Pro.

Dream it. Believe it. Do it.

Seven lessons.

One Scary Word is Deadlines.

One Latin Phrase :: Nulla dies sine linea.

One Guiding Decision :: Plot it.

One Ancient Greek :: Aristotle Rocks Characters.

One Simple Injunction :: Writer's Block Doesn't Exist.

One Slice of Advice :: Let it Sleep.

One Resolution :: Be a Writer.

Class over.

Thank You!

As always, thank you for reading this little manual. If you found it helpful, please share with other writers who are struggling with their journeys from newbies to gonnabes to professionals.

.~.~.~.

Since writing this little manual, I have created a companion writer's planner with these lessons as the guiding action plan.

It's a planner: days in a weekly spread with monthly, seasonal, and yearly reviews.

On the weekly spread you will find an inspiring quotation, areas for notes, places to record your word counts, a progress meter, a planned creative exercise on the required day off from the primary project, and healthy habits.

The monthly and seasonal reviews keep a check on your primary project as well as briefly keeping track of your secondary one. Personally, I have found that a weekly check of my progress goals is a time-sink drag. Monthly, however, that check is not a drag. The seasonal review keeps me focused and allows an opportunity to re-think my goals.

In addition to the opening goal setting is a more extended (but not time-consuming) yearly review and preview.

The planner is undated, so you can start anytime.

Our tendency is to think in calendar years. The academic calendar ruled me for several years until I rebelled.

When I decided to embark on my own publication journey, it was mid-October. Although I mulled over my journey for several weeks, I didn't really ink the plan until mid-November (the Saturday before Thanksgiving). The Sunday after, the first Sunday of Advent, became my official start.

I'm glad I started when I did. Finally.

Think / Pro is the planner that would have eased the start of my journey. I didn't realize that other people might want such guidance (*I know! I'm slow!*) until I began revising this manual.

Think / Pro: a Planner for Writers is available at online distributors.

Check out More Writing Guides from M.A. Lee

The Discovering Series

Discovering Your Novel

What kind of writer are you? Planner or Plotter? Pantster? Puzzler? Muse Muffin?

Whether you use the mosaic method or a chronological one, whether you outline every scene or let the words flow, the method does not matter. What matters is the end goal.

Discovering Your Novel is the guidebook to help you overcome the Sisyphean task of first word to publication.

With the goal of completing a novel in 52 weeks, this guidebook can be tracked week by week for persistent success. Move slower or faster to achieve your goal.

- From hatching idea to character sketches and story plan, the **Foundations** and **Visioning** sections will guide your start.
- If you have a half-completed manuscript that you're lost in, use the **Visioning** and **Analysis** sections to work your way out of the labyrinth.

Like a long ball of string, multiple charts will keep track of progress. Track your progress with daily word counts recorded on the charts. All charts are available for free at the website address provided in the guidebook

- When you complete the manuscript, what do you do next? The sections on **Harvesting** and **Finishing** answer these questions as they guide you to creating a professional career as a writer.

Learn the devices and definitions that pro writers have swirling in their heads. Maintain the discipline and preparation that keeps pro writers at work, no matter the interruptions.

If you're tired of gatekeepers and you're eager to jump on the self-publishing juggernaut, then *Discovering Your Novel* will give the guidance you need.

Discovering Characters

Developing characters is like investigating a house we want to buy.

No, I'm serious. Characters have an exterior façade that we comment upon as we drive past. Through the windows we catch glimpses of interior lives.

Even in cookie-cutter boxy cliques, characters have individual characteristics, just as the suburbia ranch houses have their garden plantings and the urban row houses have their painted doorways. These small touches create individual homes.

Characters & houses—each have individual personalities. As writers, we capture these individual characters and save them from the cookie-cutter boxy stereotypes.

We delve into interior rooms for glimpses of formative baggage. Finding their backstory is a search through attics and cellars, storage closets and garages. Characters hide their pain and fears, painting them over and adding distracting artwork.

Discovering Characters is designed to help writers find the exteriors and interiors, public and private. Five areas comprise this guidebook. Just as characters—and houses—are individual, this info is individual. You won't need every bit. Dip in and out, skim around. When you reach locked rooms, come back and explore to discover the keys to your characters.

1. Starting Points ~ offering templates and character interviews
2. Classifications ~ common and uncommon ways of discovering characters
3. Relationships ~ couples, teams, allies, enemies, mentors, etc.
4. Special Touches ~ progressions, transgressions, and transitions for character arcs
5. Significant Lists ~ archetypal characters and much more

Discovering Characters, with 44,000-plus words, is the second book in the **Discovering** set, part of the **Think like a Pro Writer** series for writers wanting to improve their game.

Discovering Plot

What do writers *want* from plot?

What do writers *need* from plot?

Are those questions the same? Not really.

As wordsmiths, we writers know that *want* and *need* are two different words.

- The ***want*** is a circumstance that we writers can control. We want plot specifics to help us craft story *and* exceed reader expectations.
- The ***need*** is a circumstance of obligations from reader expectations of story. While readers may want the comfort of the genre elements (the tropes), they also wish to have their interest and curiosity piqued.

Can we writers deliver on the expectations and the surprises in order to please our readers?

That's the involved question that *Discovering Your Plot* hopes to answer.

This guidebook covers plot structure and the necessities of genre expectations so we writers can anticipate what readers want.

- It is **NOT** a list of tropes by genre or even a list of tropes that every novel should have.

It explores the six most common plot structures.

- It is **NOT** a list of characters for plot or story. It is not a list of the "17 characters your novel needs" or the "characters used by famous authors", as listed on social media sites.

It is a detailed examination of the major sections of a novel.

- It is **NOT** a word-based or page-based formula of a novel's structure.

By the end of *Discovering Your Plot,* writers will have the tools to construct a story as well as diagnose problems with pacing, tension and suspense, and sequencing events.

Discovering Your Author Brand

The #1 marketing decision for writers is the development of a Brand.

Writers create brands for a book, for a series, and for themselves. Brands are contract with the reader, identifying quality work with artistic effort. They are a Stamp of Approval for the reader.

While everyone talks about brands and branding, few people can explain how to develop a brand.

Hopefully, *Discovering Your Author Brand* will give the guidance that writers need to develop their own brands.

First, this little guidebook is **packed with examples** based on highly successful writers. We explore these examples with step-by-step instructions to follow.

Second, we understand that the browsing readers only give a few nanoseconds to search for new books and new authors. We explain these **three main glances** that hook readers as well as the **keys to unlock** those glances. With the right keys and charts, the brand is revealed, and the door to the reader opens.

Third, we offer a third way to catch the attention of that browsing reader: **Video trailers.** Advertising claims that consumers have to see something seven times before they'll buy. Static ads and promo posts are all well and good, but we writers need an extra oomph to get that seventh look. Enter the video trailer.

We have an easily adaptable script as well as guidance on settling the debate between music and narration.

Discovering Sentence Craft

In the forests of words that we writers grow, blazed trails mark the way to our destination. Without those trails, without paths leading down to sun-sparkled streams, without the yellow brushstroke painted on tree after tree, we might lose our direction and our sanity.

Reading through that opening paragraph, most writers will recognize the extended hiking metaphor. Many will spot inversion and alliteration. A few will appreciate the anaphora and auxesis and zeugma, even when not familiar with those terms.

This is **Sentence Craft**. Controlled use creates appreciative readers. Overblown use drives readers away.

- Sentence Craft—from easy imagery to involved structures—is essential for the **poet**.
- Bloggers and other **nonfiction** writers will find it a marketing tool, distinguishing them from their competition.
- Speech writers and great broadcast journalists use these devices to make their **spoken words** become memorable.
- With **fiction**, writers paint expositions and settings and character tags, capturing readers who may not even recognize the sweeping stroke of the magical wand.

Discovering Sentence Craft is for writers new and old. For *newbies*, word-tricks can be fascinating ventures into an unknown forest. These tricks can renew a *veteran* writer's love of words and sentences flowing onto the page.

In small offerings, of course. Too many tricks glaze our readers' eyes.

Discovering Sentence Craft covers figurative and interpretive concepts as well as the structural elements that build meaning, emphasis, and memory.

Old Geeky Greeks: Write Stories with Ancient Techniques

The first writers developed techniques to influence their audiences and laid a foundation for writers today. Many techniques of these old geeky Greeks are still in use, re-packaged as glittery infographics and Wham-Pow webinars, three-point seminars and exclusive insights to *Buy Now*!

Old Geeky Greeks: Write Stories with Ancient Techniques presents techniques such as the Blood Tragedy and *dulce et utile* in a clear, organized method for writers who want to write rather than invest hours getting three snippets of information.

Chapters in *OGG* cover understanding characters to the five stages that established the modern protagonist from the ancient hero.

Aristotle's requirements for plot precede a survey of the oldest plot formula, the Blood (or Revenge) Tragedy.

Concepts such as *in medias res* and *the Tripart Being* can help writers solve sticky plot problems and develop new ideas for characterization.

Old Geeky Greeks (and Romans) tried to understand the writing that emerged from the chaos. They looked at successful plays and other story-telling methods to determine what influenced the audience.

Which characters were still talked about weeks and months after a performance? Which play structures failed—and which were consistently winners? Which ideas helped writers develop their celebrated writings?

Writers today are still searching for the answers to these questions.

The bright minds of Classical Antiquity first explored these questions, and their answers are applicable in the age of the internet, open-source software, special effects, and infographics.

Aristotle, Seneca, Plato, Horace, and many other ancient geeks have their ideas matched to Harry Potter, *Avatar, Last of the Mohicans,* and

Shakespeare.

Whether we're writing novels or plays, blogs or non-fiction, poems and songs, *Old Geeky Greeks* is a seminar in 28,000 words.

Fiction from M.A. Lee

The Into Death Series

Digging into Death ~ A governess seeking refuge, a handsome young man, an archaeological dig: the situation is ripe for romance.

Yet when love blossoms between between Isabella and Madoc, a murder soon happens. Suspicions escalate. Artifacts are stolen. Then a second murder occurs.

Has the love of Isabella's life beguiled her straight into death?

Christmas with Death ~ Christmas is for miracles, merriment, and murder.

Isabella and her friends attend a Christmastide party at an English country manor. When murder occurs, will Isabella or her friends be blamed?

Or will one of them be the next victim?

Portrait with Death ~ Isabella travels to a country village to finish a commission. There she befriends the young photographer Flick Sherborne. Then murder intrudes when they stumble upon the body of George Webberly, a teacher at the local prep school. He's been bludgeoned to death.

Why would anyone kill a school master? Motives abound, and suspects increase. Who committed the murder? Can Isabella find the answer?

Or will a murderer paint with more blood?

Into Death, a bundle of *Digging into Death, Christmas with Death,* and *Portrait with Death.*

Coming Soon: short stories featuring Isabella on a passenger ship to join her husband in India

The Hearts in Hazard series

Loosely-connected novels in Regency England

1 ~ *A Game of Secrets* ~ Smugglers, secrets and spies: Kate tries to hide in plain sight; Tony tries to catch a spy. First they fall in love; then they fall into trouble with smugglers. Will they survive?

2 ~ *A Game of Spies* ~ Salons and soirées, flirtation and dancing, gambling and spies: Josette and Giles fall in love over a deck of cards and try not to die.

3 ~ *A Game of Hearts* ~ Two couples :: Rafe & Maggie ~ One titled widow, one wealthy businessman: two hearts shadowed by their past. Connie & Roger ~ One bright young flirt, one hard-edged young man: two hearts crossed by circumstance. Mix in a courtesan and two rakes, all out for mischief, and murder bloody and foul.

A Trio of Games, a bundle of *A Game of Secrets, A Game of Spies,* and *A Game of Hearts*

4 ~ *The Danger of Secrets* ~ Deep in the wintry countryside, a house warmed by relatives and friends: secrets of family, secrets of hearts, secrets of blood and pain. Match a daughter to an unknown father; match a spinster to an earl; match a serial killer to his next victim.

5 ~ *The Danger for Spies* ~ Impossible: rakes don't lose their hearts. Impossible: spies don't give up the game. Impossible: no one hides in plain sight. Impossible: codes are unbreakable. Impossible: a man can't hold onto revenge for years and years. Impossibilities are designed to be shattered.

6 ~ *The Danger to Hearts* ~ A country manor in early Spring: older woman and younger man. Horses, cats, needlework, roses and afternoon teas ~ what could possibly go wrong in an idyll? Trouble in the past, trouble now, and murder.

A Trio of Dangers, a bundle of *The Danger of Secrets, The Danger for Spies,* and *The Danger to Hearts*

7 ~ *The Key to Secrets* ~ Debutantes should snare fiancés, not murder them. Constable Hector Evans (from *The Danger to Hearts)* returns to solve three murders. Is his former love guilty or a convenient scapegoat?

8 ~ *The Key for Spies* ~~ Love changes loyalties. Simon Pargeter, in Spain as a reconnaissance officer for General Wellesley, encounters Miriella, leader of guerrillas fighting the French. Will Miri risk helping the British officer spy? Or will she sacrifice him in order to save her family and home and men?

9 ~ *The Key with Hearts* ~~A convenient marriage inconveniently causes murder. Married for money, not for love, who can Beth trust? Will she be the next victim?

A Trio of Keys, a bundle of *The Key to Secrets, The Key for Spies,* and *The Key for Hearts*

10 ~ *The Hazard of Secrets* ~ Two hearts with dangerous pasts ~ Can they keep their secrets, or will murder force them to reveal all? Fate brings these two lonely souls together. Chance helps them escape. Will murder bring a bloody solution?

11 ~ *The Hazard for Spies* ~ Disguised to Spy. The young Constable Conrad Hoppock tracks treacherous traitors. Spinster Phinney Darracott hopes to find a killer. Will murder destroy their chance for love?

12 ~ *The Hazard with Hearts* ~ The new bride to the Earl of Sheldrake, Vivienne Northrup claims to be too rational to believe in ghosts. Yet two wives haunt Sheldrake Hall. Will Vivienne become the third wife to die?

Her husband Max Herrick lost two brides tragically, the first to suicide, the second to an accident. Or were they murdered? Is he a Bluebeard, killing his wives, one after another?

A Trio of Hazards, a bundle of *The Hazard of Secrets, The Hazard for Spies,* and *The Hazard for Hearts*

Read on for a Teaser from "The Lion's Den", a Stand-Alone Short Story. Set in 1920

"The Lion's Den" ~ Jack Portman had never forgotten Filly Malvaise. Then she walked into his local pub and into the clutches of a loan shark. Can he rescue her before she falls victim to evil?

"The Lion's Den"

Hell and damnation.

Jack Portman lifted the pint of stout to hide his face and watched Filly Malvaise look around the pub. That had to be her fourth look, just as blind as the previous ones. Not all of them would be blind.

He hadn't forgotten her, not a single jot. She'd changed, though. Up with the times, in one of those head-covering hats, her hair bobbed. The loss of her long brown hair hit him like a punch. She wore a shapeless serge grey jacket over a dress. The skirt revealed her calves. That skirt almost made up for her cut hair.

Jack had spotted Filly as soon as she entered the pub. She had threaded her way through the early Wednesday evening crowd of clerks and office jobsmen and a light sprinkling of women. A small table in the center caught her eye, and she slid onto the rattan-backed chair. No sooner had she planted herself than a man placed his hand on the other chair. Jack wanted to hit him. Brown eyes wide, Filly gave a decided shake of her head. The man dragged out the chair anyway. Her gloved hand shot out in a warding gesture. Whatever she said wiped the grin off the man's face. He rejoined his mates at a larger side table and mouthed a word. Looked like *married*.

Which Jack knew was an effing lie.

He might not have seen Filly Bedamned Malvaise for three years, but he'd listened for information about her. He'd known when she moved to London and took rooms from the widowed Cecilia Arkwright before she became the married Cecilia Tarrant. He knew she'd found work at a dress shop.

Jack watched her give an order to the barmaid. Her upturned face caught the lamp's glare. When the maid departed, she looked around the pub.

Something troubled her. Whatever had brought her to his local. The Gold Eagle Pub was far from her flat and her work.

They were up to five looks, still blind.

Occasionally, Filly ran with the other Bright Young Things, the racy ones who jumped in fountains with her cousin Tori or the Bohemian ones who talked around paintings and sculpture with her cousin Greta. Tori and Greta ordered around anyone in their circles. Filly didn't take their orders, which put her in the outer sphere, for all the blood connection.

He'd like her from the start, that Christmas at Emberley, the Malvaise estate—although her father was second son and had inherited only a modicum of wealth. Still, a modicum was more than Jack had. Filly hadn't panicked when Tony Gresham turned up murdered. She hadn't tried to interfere with the investigation. Plucky thing had stood up to her cousins' interferences.

Jack had thought her too young. His years in the sodding trenches aged him, mental years rather than physical years. He had a need to earn his pay rather than live off the Malvaise family.

Filly Bedamned Malvaise wasn't effing married, though.

The barmaid returned with two pints, one for Filly, one for whomever she'd come to meet.

Married.

Shite. How had he missed that news?

She sipped the beer and grimaced.

Jack should leave. He had an early day tomorrow. His job required a clear head, clear thinking and quick reactions.

He stayed to see who came to her table. He didn't see Filly seeking out a pub on her own. She fit a tea room.

She unsnapped her purse and withdrew a lace handkerchief. She dabbed her pinkened mouth to remove the beer foam. Jack drank his stout while she rummaged in her purse. She drew out a man's pocket watch and opened it to check the time. Then the watch and the hanky returned to the purse, and she snapped it shut. She expectantly watched the door where thugs monitored who entered the Gold Eagle.

A man bumped past Jack. The man didn't bother to apologize, just headed around the bar.

Jack took one look at the mustached profile, the smashed nose, and round spectacles under bushy eyebrows.

Oh, hell no.

Boggs. Thaddeus Boggs, the arsehole. Filly wasn't in debt to him, was she?

Boggs came from the back, employees only. That made Jack rethink his choice of local. The arsehole wrapped his thick fingers around whoever he could then squeezed and squeezed until they choked up whatever he wanted.

And he plonked down in the chair across from Filly Bedamned Malvaise.

Hell and damnation.

She didn't smile. Jack would have cursed aloud if she had. She could have ruined all his dreams with one sweet curve of her pinked lips. But she didn't smile at Boggs.

She frowned.

Boggs grinned. His tongue touched his upper lip as he listened. Then he shook his head. Whatever he replied widened Filly's brown eyes.

Then Boggs wrapped his fat fingers around the pint and stood. His other hand swept out, an obvious gesture for her to precede him. She hesitated. Boggs said something short. Filly's dislike couldn't be mistaken, but she stood and looked over at the bar's corner.

Right at Jack.

His nearly empty pint of stout still hid his face.

Yet she wasn't looking at him. She spied the swinging door behind him and started for it. Boggs followed, enjoying the view he had of Filly's legs in low heels.

She passed within inches of Jack. Boggs came right behind her.

And Jack intended to find out what shady business Filly had with a moneylender like Thaddeus Boggs.

He waited until the barkeep shifted down the bar to pour a cluster of pints. Then Jack slipped back the half-yard needed to step against then through the swinging door.

The shadowed hall lacked the yellow glaring light of the pub. Light streamed around the door directly opposite, a kitchen by the sounds leaking through. At the hall's end was a heavy door with two locks, the side door. On the way down to it were two more doors. Pubside would be the coze, no longer in use. Opposite it, a little further along, was another door.

Jack tried the knob to the coze. It turned easily. The door swung into darkness, street lights shining through the windows, the bottom halves blocked by curtains so the people in booths had privacy. He left the coze door ajar and soft-footed to the opposite door.

Pale light streamed under the door. He heard Filly before he reached the door.

"—gone up? Why has the price gone up?"

"I said it does. Fair market price."

"Fair?"

Hell and damnation. Why had she gone to a moneylender?

"Bidding war," Boggs said.

"You had a deal."

"Like I said then, one time offer. Gone now. Price went up. And up again."

"What do you mean? What do you mean by bidding war?"

"Someone else wants it. They've offered more."

"How much more?"

"I want £400. From you."

"Four—? I don't have that much. I brought the agreed price. I don't think we can get more."

"We can make that the down payment. Sweeten the deal."

Jack didn't like that oily insinuation.

"Sweeten it how?"

"You. Now."

Jack reached for the door.

"Or her. Tomorrow night. All the night. Matter of fact, I like that idea more."

"She won't agree to that." Filly's voice shook, fear or rage. "And what guarantee do we have that you will not raise the price again?"

"That's a chance you take. Like I said, he offers more, the price will go up and up."

More Titles from Writers Ink Books

From Remi Black

The **Fae-Mark'd Wizard** series, novels of epic fantasy :: A wizard banished. Sorcery wrecking evil. Wyre and wraiths enslaved to sorcerers.

Weave a Wizardry Web ~ A wyre pack begins hunting wizards. Alstera practices a forbidden magical linkage one time too many. Will she survive her chosen road?

Dream a Deadly Dream ~ Assassination. A fugitive comtesse. A lethal sleep-spell. A sorcerous plot to kill the king weaves together past and present, dream and reality, to create a nightmare that kills. On a mission to redeem herself, can Alstera stop the dreams before the Comtesse is killed?

Sing a Graveyard Song ~ Can Alstera defeat Death Walking before it takes yet another life? Or will wielding blood-magic against a blood-spelled creature force Alstera across the tenuous barrier that separates wizardry from foul sorcery?

Dance to Bone-Edged Music (coming soon)

Tangled Spells ~ a bundle of the first three novels in the **Fae Mark'd Wizard** series.

The **Fae Mark'd World** series, novellas of action-adventure fantasy. Elemental magic. Cold steel. Twisted sorcery. Magical monsters.

Spells of Air

To Wield the Wind

On a mission for the Wizard Enclave, Orielle ventures into the Wilding, a strange frontier filled with magical creatures. There she discovers sprites and wraiths, gobbers and wyre. All view her as prey.

To Charm the Air

When Orielle and Grim reach the Haven, the elder arrests Grim. The Haveners aren't interested in a renewed alliance with the Wizard Enclave.

Is her mission for the Enclave in vain? Will she ever escape the Wilding? Or will wraiths consume her?

To Curse the Wyre

The sorceress and her servants, the shifter wyre, seek to destroy Orielle's allies in the Wilding. Orielle has gathered Dark Fae and Rhoghieri to defeat them.

She rides with the Dark Fae Lord Skull and Lady Bone—but can she trust them?

Spells of Earth

The Wyrded Earth

With death menacing, Desora has little protection except her wards. Wolfen and an eldritch monster kill the defenseless. Can Desora discover powerful ways to wield Earth before she becomes monstrous prey?

The Riven Gate

Captain Brax, his guards and the rangers travel with Desora to the forest palace of Horst, the Dark Fae who rules the northern Wilding. An alliance with him offers the only chance to defeat the eldritch monster. Will they survive their next encounter with the monster?

The Mysts of Sorcery

Only when the monster is destroyed will Mulgrum and the Northern Reaches be safe. The sorcerer who opened the portal that admitted the monster must also be killed.

With allies gathered, the final battle draws near. Yet betrayal rears its ugly head. Will Desora defeat her enemies and protect her friends?

Spells of Water

Torrent of Evil

Death. That was the omen that the crows and ravens brought to Inkeri.

Deep in the desert Idros Ahdreide, men had lost their lives in battle against a strange evil. A half-Fae wielder, Inkeri ventures to investigate with Rhodren, baron of the Bois Argent, and his troop.

The Ahdreide has predators aplenty, all willing to feast on the wariest of travelers. What enemy marshals these dangers? What evil lurks in the desert?

Storm of Spells (coming soon)

Venom of Dragons (coming soon)

from Edie Roones

the **Wild Sherwood** series ~ exploits featuring the legendary outlaws of Sherwood Forest and others, melded with the dangerous Faeries of British myth

Into Wild Sherwood (five short stories in a collaboration with M.A. Lee)

"Tod the Fox and the Faeries in the Ring" ~ *Never enter a Faerie Ring. The Faeries like to play.* How can Tod escape them?

"The Poisoner and the Faerie Huntsman" ~ *Never reveal weakness to a Faerie.* Melly and her hound encounter strange black hounds. Then the Huntsman of the Wild Hunt arrives. Has she fallen into greater trouble?

"Three Yule Feasts for the Faeries" ~ *Will the cook become the final dish?* A Faerie sentinel tempts Ellen to cook three dinners. For each, she'll receive three purses, copper and silver and gold. But what does the Faerie mean by *final* feast?

"Friar Tuck and the Faerie at the Pool" ~ *Faeries are wondrous, strange, and deadly.* When Friar Tuck is trapped by the Faerie at the pool, can he convince her that he is a man of peace?

"Alan-a-Dale and the Harp of Elandrielle" ~ *Who can trust a Faerie?* At his lowest point, a Faerie finds Alan and offers her aid. Should he accept her bargain?

Outlaws of Wild Sherwood (five more short stories in a collaboration with M.A. Lee)

"A Twist of Faerie Magic" ~ *A twist of murder. A twist of Faerie magic. And Dav the wrestler caught between.* When Dav is accused of murdering his true love's husband, will magic reveal the true culprit?

"A Faerie Song for a Feast" ~ *Masks, Mummers, and a Faerie Song.* Alan-a-Dale risks playing a song learned in the land of Faeries to help Robin Hood and his men. Will the song help or hinder the outlaws?

"Mischief of a Faerie" ~ *A Challenge with Quarterstaves.* When his sister names a bearded giant as her newborn's father, Arthur storms off to force

Little John to support them. Yet how can a simple poacher defeat a man taller and stronger than he is?

"The Green Man" ~ *A Venture with Destiny*. Bad luck has plagued Jack Greenleaf for years. Abandoned, evicted, and rejected, he joined the other outcasts in Sherwood Forest. The Green Man of the Faerie may seal his fate.

"The Prize of a Golden Arrow" ~ *By Hook or Crook or Arrow*. Gil vowed never again to take up the long bow. Then he learns the May Day archery contest is a trap to capture Robin Hood. He resolves to foil the Sheriff's plan.

Arrows of Wild Sherwood

The Hooded Outlaw ~ One trap for Robin Hood, another for Lady Marianne. The corrupt Sheriff of Nottingham and a local baron plot to arrest Robin Hood and to steal land from Lady Marianne's family. How can outlaws and a disguised Faerie prevent the traps?

The Rogue of Sherwood ~ coming soon

The Knife of Sherwood ~ coming soon

The Great Heart of the Forest ~ coming soon

The **Seasons in Sansward** Quarternary ~ High Fantasy Novels

Summer Sieges ~ The sole survivor of a fierce battle, Warder Beren escapes the Watrani horde and their allies the Gitane Witches. Aided by an enchanted red wolf, she returns to her castlekeep with the Watrani on her heels.

Foul sorcery and twisted monsters confront her. The road to safety is narrow and dangerous, shadowed and terrifying. What sacrifices will be needed to escape the Watrani and Gitane?

Autumn Spells ~ A dark dame wields sorcery to extend her life unnaturally. She needs two innocent souls for her spells to succeed.

Unaware of her evil workings, the green mage Saisha befriends the castellan Hethan. When they fall into the dark dame's trap, can they escape the spell before it damages them? Or must they venture into the shadowy tower the dark dame controls to destroy the spell and the dark dame?

Winter Sorcery ~ Cover blown, the two Frenc spies Rolf and Catal stumble upon the very sphere of power they have sought. The Kaerrefiorne increases the sorcery wielded by Gitane Witches. The spies steal the sphere then run for their lives across the wintry plains. In close pursuit are a Gitane Witchmaster and a troop of Watrani.

Only two people help Rolf and Catal. The half-trained mage Niijai and a temple cleric Legeeta offer them shelter and a hiding place. Yet the arrival of their enemies traps them all. Suspicions and sorcery are closing a trap. How can the spies escape with the sphere?

Spring Magicks (in the sketching stage)

Index ~ References are to Chapters

4-act movement
60
5-act play structure
58
5 Rules for Writing
35
5-step writing plan
38
5,000- Words an Hour 110
6 thinking hats 112
7 Habits of Highly Influential People
46
7 in 7 111
7 work steps
26
10 factors for a project 16
12 key pillars
17

ally
92
Amazon Kindle Revolution 129
antagonist 23, 78
Antigone
70
Apelles 33, 97
archetypal
story pattern
62
Atonement
48
Austen, Jane
50
Mansfield Park
82
Northanger Abbey
50

"Beauty & the Beast"
54
Bell, James Scott
64
Benchley, Peter
47
Benton, Robert 54
Best Exotic Marigold Hotel, the
50
block, writer's
86
blocking figures
22
Bonnie and Clyde
54
de Bono, Edward 112
Booker, Christopher
45
break away 95 &
ff
Bryson, Bill
52
budget see Tax Tips
Buzan, Tony 108

calendar for writing 18, 38
Carnegie, Dale
38
cameo
22
Campbell, Joseph
62
catastrophe
75
catharsis
76
chorus
82

Christmas Carol, a
55
"Cinderella"
48
Cleeves, Ann
84
Clinical depression			104
coincidence
84
collage			26, 108, 111
comedy
45
confidante
21
conflict, 5 forms
81
cost analysis			114
Covey, Stephen
46
Criticism vs. critique			101
cure-alls
89
credits/debits   see Tax Tips
Czikszentmihali,		Mihaly
46

de Bono, Edward			112
de   Villeneuve,   G-S   Barbot
54
deadline
13
delay vs. procrastination
98
depression			102
depression, clinical			104
deuteragonist
78
deux ex machina
84
devil's advocate … see *judge*
diagnostic quiz
90

Dickens, Charles
55
drafting
37
dream writing			109
Duarte, Nancy
60
dulce et utile
76

Eat, Pray, Love
54
Editing			19, 37
Emotion (thinking hat)			112
Equipment		see Tax Tips
escape
91
escape exercise
92
Estes, Clarissa P.			104
expenses/earnings   see Tax Tips

failure			100
fear (for characters)
78
*Five   Thousand   Words   an
    Hour*			110
Financial Peace
46
flash fiction			110
Flow
46
foil
22
Fox, Chris			110
foreshadowing
85
free-writing			109
Freytag's Pyramid
57

genre switch			110

ghosts (character)
78
Good Deeds
49

habits, healthy   102
hamartia
73
Hamlet   57-
60
Harry Potter
74
healthy habits   102
Heinlein, Robert
35
Hemingway, Ernest   110
Henry V   57-
60
Heresy, writing
86
Hero's Journey
62
Hobbit, the
51
Homer
51
Horace
76
hubris
73

idol
83
Indiana Jones
73
income/outgo   see Tax Tips
Ingledew, John   110
irony   25, 73

Jaws
47

155

Jobs, Steve
60
Johnson, Spencer
46
jokester
83
journal   109
judge (thinking hat)   112
judgment   101
juggling   118

key pillars
17
King, Martin Luther Jr.
60
Knolling
111

logic (thinking hat)
112
London, Jack   opening page
love interest
83

McCarthy, Cormac
23
McEwan, Ian
48
McKim, Bob   110
McKinley, Robin
23
Macbeth   57-
60
man vs. (5 types)
81
Mansfield Park
82
mantra   33, 118
master book   25, 30
Medea   70, 79 &
ff
Midsummer Night's Dream, a 57ff
mileage   see Tax Tips

mimesis
71
mind map	108
miscellaneous expenses
see Tax Tips
Moggach, Deborah
50
Monster / overcoming the
45
Much Ado About Nothing	57-60

NaNoWriMo	28 &
ff
Newman, David
54
Nin, Anaïs
34
Northanger Abbey
50

observation scenario	110
Odyssey
51
office supplies	see Tax Tips
operating equipment
see Tax Tips
operating expenses
see Tax Tips
optimism (thinking hat)	112
organization	97, 112
Orwell, George	opening page
overcoming the monster	51-53
overwhelmed
94

pantster	63 &
ff
perfect person
82
peripeteia
73

Perry, Tyler
49
planning	36 &
ff
Plot 7	17, 23 &
ff
plotter	...63 &
ff
procrastination
98
professional expenses.see Tax
Tips
professionalism	121 &
ff
progress meter	130
project factors
16
proofing
37
protagonist	21 &
ff

quest
45
quiz
90

rags to riches
45
Raiders of the Lost Ark	46, 73
Ramsey, Dave
46
rebirth
54
revising
37
rhetorical devices
28
Romeo & Juliet	57-60 & *ff*
Rowling, JK
74
Rules for Writing
35

scenario from observation 110
secrets (character)
78
seeming ally 22, 84
sentence structures
28
Seven Habits of Highly Influential People
46
Shakespeare, William 57-60 & ff
Plays Discussed
Hamlet
Henry V
Macbeth
Midsummer Night's Dream
Much Ado about Nothing
his play structure
Romeo & Juliet
shapeshifter
84
side characters 82, 83
sketching 36, 38
sleep on it 111
slime 102, 104
Smith, Dean Wesley 66, 110
Spann, Susan
41
stagnation 102, 104
Standard American English
38
Stewart, Mary
28
storyboard 112
Super Structure
64
Supplies see Tax Tips
switch genres 110

tagline 19, 38, 55, 95
Tax Tips
122

Teaser see Theme
TED Talk
60
Theme 19, 38, 55, 95
thinking hats 112
threshold guardian
84
tilt sideways 109
Tolkien, JRR
51
Tolstoy, Leo
37
Tragedy
45
trickster
83
tritagonist
79
troll 101
Trollope, Anthony
37

Under the Tuscan Sun
54

Vera
84
de Villeneuve, G-S B
54
Vogler, Christopher
62
voyage & return
50

Walk in the Woods, a
52
walk-ons
22
Wild 54, 84
Windig, Chuck 31. 41
Who Moved my Cheese?
46

Women Who Run with the Wolves 104
word counts 16, 130
work steps 26
writer's block 9, 86 & *ff,* 127
Writer's Journey, the 62
Writing Into the Dark 66, 110
writing plan 38
writing rules 35
writing sprints 110

Zinsser, William opening page

Notes

Notes

Notes

Notes